accelerated learning

FIRST FUNDAMENTALS™

Designed, developed and published by
Accelerated Learning
Systems Ltd.

Written by Gordon Dryden
Project conceived and directed by Colin Rose

Edited by Malcolm J. Nicholl and Colin Rose

Illustrated by Mick Davis

Production assistants: Maria Blank and Anne Kenyon

First published 1995
Reprinted 1996

ISBN 0 905553 46 2

Contents

Foreword

Accelerated Learning First FUNdamentals is for parents of babies from birth through to the age of 18 months. It is designed as the introduction to a unique, complete child development program called *Accelerated Learning FUNdamentals*. This latter program will help you develop your child's potential from about 18 months to six years.

> *The principle goal of education is to help people be capable of new things, not simply repeat what other generations have done — people who are creative, inventive and discoverers.*
>
> Jean Piaget

Both *First FUNdamentals* and *FUNdamentals* were created to a clear vision. The vision is that your child should grow up to have truly rounded capabilities and, above all, to be happy.

I put the highest possible value on the word 'rounded.' What would be the point, for example, of helping your child to read early or to be very numerate, if she* lacked curiosity, creativity or a delight in nature? Or did not possess the ability to share generously, relate well and cooperate with others?

I also put a high value on the word 'planned.' To work to a plan doesn't mean you lack spontaneity, laughter or fun. It merely means that you not only have a dream for your child; but you also have thought out how best to achieve that dream. It's a structured, not a haphazard, development.

The pyramid of happiness

> *The child is the father of the man.*
>
> William Wordsworth

It may feel a little strange to look at your tiny baby and think in detail about his future. Nothing great, however, is achieved without a plan.

I like to visualize a child's early development as a series of foundation stones and building blocks that need to be put in place, step-by-step, starting with the basics, in order to achieve the ultimate goal of happiness. This pyramid structure is the plan on which the entire *FUNdamentals* program is based.

I'm not assuming that you will agree with all the elements in this pyramid. All parents will have their own ideas and additions—spirituality and sense of humor for example. But parents must build these in their own way.

The pyramid is merely a way to visualize the complex inter-relationship between the abilities, characteristics and values that combine to make up ultimate happiness and success.

The *FUNdamentals* program that covers the ages from 18 months to six years will help you develop the building blocks, characteristics and values that form the upper levels of the pyramid. *First FUNdamentals* is designed to help you start to put the foundation stones into place.

> *Children are travelers in an unknown land and we are their guides.*
>
> Robert Fisher

Let's look briefly at each of those foundation stones.

** Apologies to your child. For simplicity, we switch between the sexes throughout this book, so sometimes it's 'he' and sometimes 'she.'*

Essential building blocks for a happier, brighter child

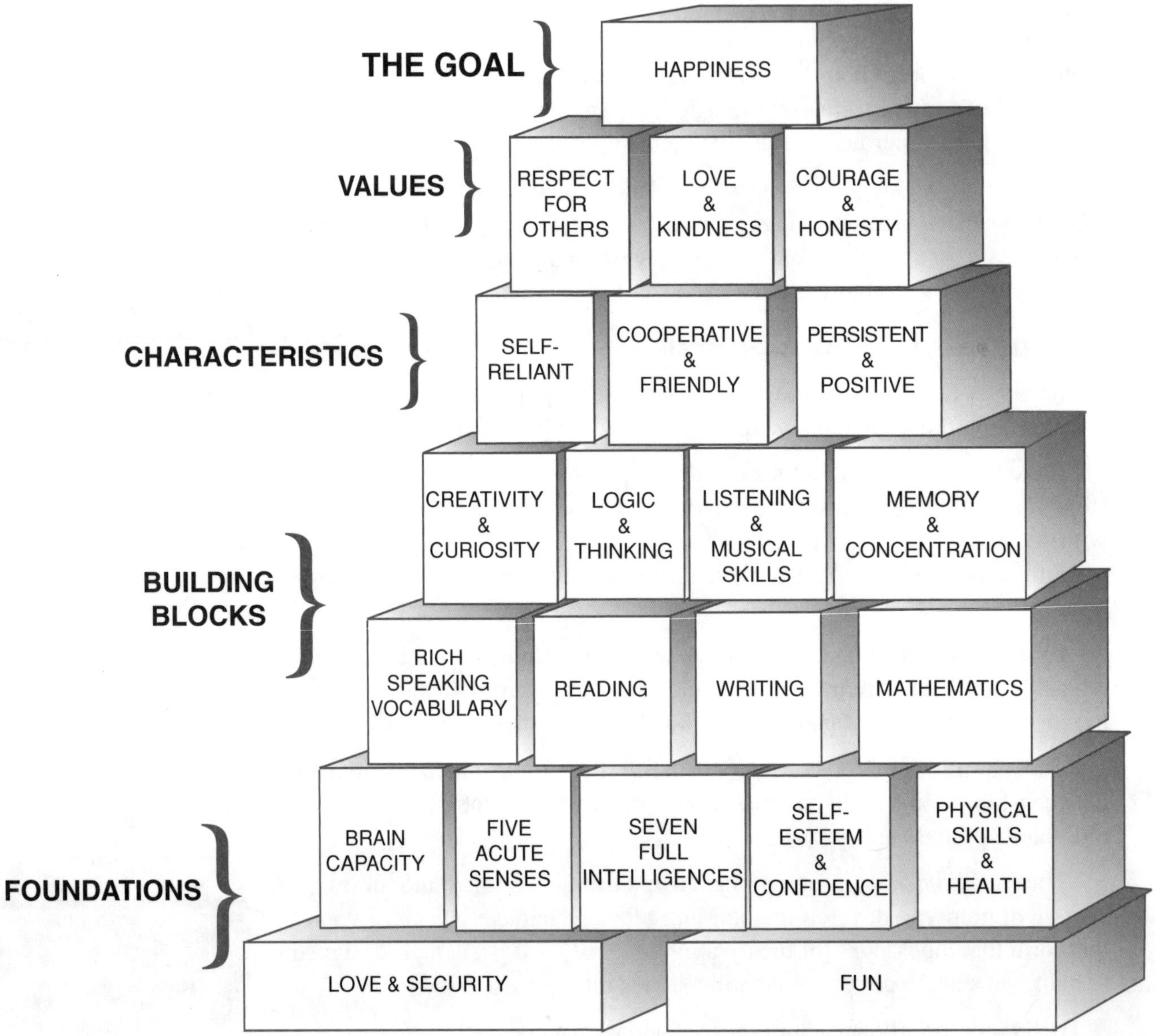

Underpinning it all is the **love and security** you provide. **Nothing** is more important. You'll see later in this Guidebook that insecurity and threat actually prevent your child's brain from working properly. Love and security, on the other hand, actually release chemicals that make the brain work better.

> *A child's life is like a piece of paper on which everyone who passes by leaves an impression.*
>
> Chinese Proverb

So does **fun**. That's why this program is based mainly on games and activities. But while they are lots of fun, they all have a purpose. They each contribute to one or more of the building blocks. There is a big difference between fun, 'purposeful play,' and activities that merely fill time.

When you play a game from *First FUNdamentals* you can be sure it is contributing directly to either your child's physical, emotional or intellectual development. Hence the double emphasis in naming our program ***FUN*** *da* ***mentals***.

Brain building. You'll learn in this Guidebook that your child is born with more than enough brain cells to be highly successful. It's not the number of brain cells that determines usable intelligence, it's the number of **connections** that are made **between** those brain cells.

These connections are formed by the experiences and thoughts that you prompt for your child through the rich, stimulating environment you provide in the early years.

> *We used to think that play and education were opposite things. Now we know better. Educational experts and early childhood specialists have discovered that play is learning and, even more, that play is one of the most effective kinds of learning.*
>
> Jean Marzolla and Janice Lloyd in *Learning Through Play*

The illustration below says it all. What you do with this program will **directly** affect your child's brain capacity.

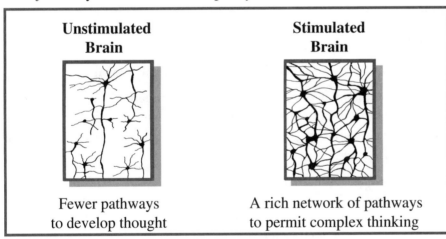

Unstimulated Brain | **Stimulated Brain**

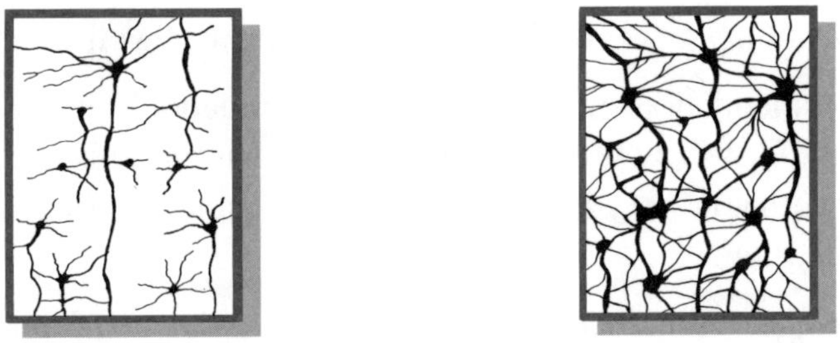

Fewer pathways to develop thought | A rich network of pathways to permit complex thinking

Five acute senses. Your child learns through his senses. So activities that build strong senses are vital to enable him to learn better, as well as get more pleasure from life.

> *Nothing is more fundamental to solid educational development than pure uncontaminated curiosity.*
>
> Burton L. White in *The First Three Years of Life*

Through *First FUNdamentals,* your child will learn eye-tracking skills, early musical skills, listening skills, as well as physical 'motor' skills such as finger and thumb control.

Seven full intelligences. One of the most important new insights into the brain comes from one of America's prestigious universities, Harvard. It argues that intelligence is **not** fixed.

Instead of the restrictive idea of a single fixed IQ, it shows that your child has at least seven different forms of intelligence—linguistic, mathematical-logical, musical, visual-spatial, physical, social and introspective. There's more about the different intelligences on page 12.

> *You are unique. In all the world there is no child like you.*
>
> Pablo Cassals

For your child to grow up with truly rounded abilities, she needs to develop each one of these intelligences. *FUNdamentals* shows you how to help her do this in an organized way.

Self-esteem. Like love and security, self-esteem is a vital foundation for success, but unlike love and security, which only *you* can give, a child must develop his own self-esteem.

The last foundation stone is, of course, **health and physical skills**. You will find many ideas in this program that build physical skill—including some remarkable new activities that directly build brain capacity.

A warning

> *Babies need people: talking, laughing, warm-hearted people, constantly drawing them into their lives and offering them the world for a playground.*
>
> Dorothy Butler in *Babies Need Books*

There is a big difference between a rich, stimulating, enjoyable environment —and pressure.

Over-ambitious parents fail because, instead of support and encouragement, they provide a hot-house environment and pressure. The entire *FUNdamentals* program is based on providing natural opportunities for your child to bloom.

The unshakeable rule is this: **if your child is not enjoying an activity, stop immediately**.

How the program works

First FUNdamentals is designed to be practical as well as fun.

The recommendations in this easy-to-read guidebook are designed to be just as easy to follow. But the heart of the program is the activity cards. Carry them around with you and you'll never be short of games and activities to play with your offspring.

As a bonus, we've included with your *First FUNdamentals* program cards displaying some of baby's first words to read. Yes, it's entirely possible for a baby to read words. The visual stimulation cards produced to accompany this Guidebook are a vital tool to help 'wire' baby's visual circuitry.

> *Kindergarten is too late.*
>
> Mazaru Ibuku, (co-founder of Sony) in a book of the same name

You'll find that — together — all of these tools will help to make playtime, dinnertime, bathtime, bedtime all become time well spent.

A rounded child

Let me reiterate: the central idea behind *First FUNdamentals* and its following companion — *FUNdamentals* — is to combine fun and laughter with games and activities that contribute to all-round strengths.

Although your baby is very small now and has limited means of communicating back to you, you can be sure that he takes in much, much more than it appears. And what is taken in now will eventually come out later as ability and attitude.

We are our children's first and most important teachers. The time and effort that you put into these activities and games now will be rewarded by enhanced capabilities in the future.

Children are like seeds planted in the ground. They must be watered daily. With constant care and attention, the seed will grow into a plant and eventually flower.

Shinichi Suzuki in
Nurtured by Love

A personal note

I have four children. Susan, 32, Helen, 30, Alexander $4^1/2$ and Catherine who is 14 months old. I see my two older daughters almost every day, so we are very close.

But I also know that the years in which your child will prefer to be with you, rather than playing with his friends, are all too short. So live them together to the fullest.

The activities and games you play today will build more than ability: they will build bonds and loving memories.

With best wishes for happy parenting,

Colin Rose
Editor and Project Director
July 1995

The goal of giving the infant a feeling of being cared for is, in my judgment, the single most important goal in getting a child off to a good start in life.

Burton L. White in
The First Three Years of Life

P.S. There are dozens of good activities in the main text of the Guidebook to supplement the Activity Cards. You might like to copy your favorites from the text onto cards—so you have them with you all the time.

Introduction

Often the greatest truths are the simplest. And these are among the greatest, simplest truths to emerge from 30 years of research around the world.

At least 50 percent of everyone's ability to learn is developed in the first five years of life. About 30 percent more is developed before the eighth birthday.

▲ This means that parents are the world's main teachers.

▲ Children are their own best educators.

▲ And the home, not the school, is the most important educational institution.

Yet no nation spends even one percent of its educational budget on the most vital task of all: training the parents of young children.

Just think about it. Whatever you buy — a coffee maker, a telephone, *any* simple household appliance — comes with a detailed instruction manual. Invest in a computer and you'll get a giant operations manual.

At the moment a child is born, it's already brilliant. It picks up language, much better than a doctor of philosophy in any subject, in only two years. And it is a master at it by three or four.

Tony Buzan, British psychologist

Yet, as British psychologist Tony Buzan puts it: your children arrive on earth with the world's most amazing bio-computer (the human brain) but where's the instruction manual?

Accelerated Learning First FUNdamentals program is **your** first instruction manual. It provides you, as a parent, with the information needed to give your baby a flying start in life.

Overall, it means structuring an environment in which your child can 'explode' into learning—the natural, unforced, fun-filled way.

This is not a program about developing 'hot-house babies.' It does not want you to force children to do anything they don't love and enjoy. And we are not saying that anyone absorbs 50 percent of life's *knowledge* in the first five years of life. Nor 50 percent of one's *wisdom.*

The child creates its own mental muscles . . . The discovery that the child has a mind able to absorb on its own account produces a revolution in education.

Dr. Maria Montessori, Italy's first woman doctor of medicine and founder of the Montessori method

What it simply means is that in the first five years your child forms 50 percent of the *main learning pathways* in his brain. Everything else he learns in life will be built on that base. If the base is not sound, future growth is stunted. Making brain connections gives your child an invaluable advantage.

Although the suggestions contained in the *Accelerated Learning First FUNdamentals* program are many and varied, the principles are amazingly simple. The key word is **FUN.** Fun-filled learning can be the best party in town —for both parent and child.

And it's never too early to start.

1. Developing the amazing brain

Here's one way to appreciate the staggering capacity of your baby's brain:

▲ A fruit fly has 100,000 brain cells.

▲ A mouse has five million.

▲ A monkey has 10 million.

▲ Every healthy baby is born with approximately 100 ***billion*** active brain cells, or neurons.

▲ And each cell is capable of sprouting up to 20,000 different branches to store and process information.

We now know that each one of us possesses at birth a brain potentially more powerful than the world's greatest computers—and that intelligence is not fixed.

We also know that each of us is only using a small fraction of that ability. And you can help your children to use much more. Almost every child has the potential to flower in dozens of different ways.

Here's why:

▲ The brain's most vital connections are made very early in life. They are the basis of all future learning and mental ability.

▲ These connections grow directly as a result of a child's rich and varied experiences. The activities outlined in the *First FUNdamentals* program are designed to provide precisely that stimulation at the time when it is most vital for brain growth.

▲ A healthy baby will also grow around 900 billion other cells which surround and nourish the active neurons. Exercise and good diet are vital to build and maintain the cells that provide the brain's nutrients. Proper nourishment builds a strong brain as well as a strong body.

▲ The brain communicates with the rest of the body by nerve pathways. Each pathway can transmit those messages efficiently only if it is well coated with a special insulation. When fully coated — generally by about the age of seven — each nerve pathway can send messages around the brain and body up to 150 miles an hour.

▲ The brain also has at least seven main 'processing centers.' Some now call them seven different 'intelligences.' Many people develop only one or two, to the detriment of the rest. They may be brilliant at mathematics or language but weak in music and art. Yet each one of us can develop all those abilities.

And *FUNdamentals* will help you do that with your child.

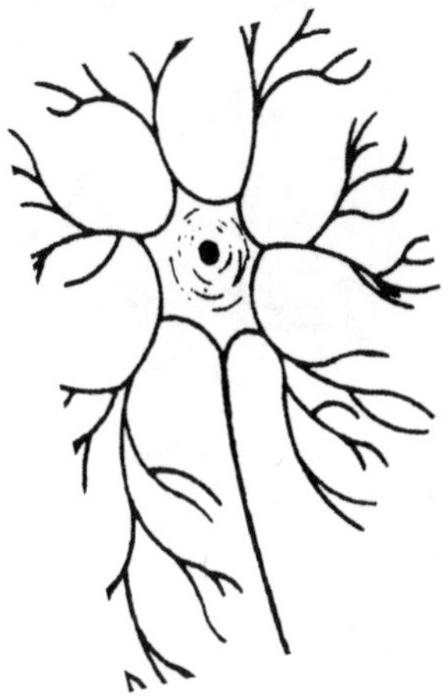

Each of your child's 100 billion brain cells starts like the circular neuron above. As the child is exposed to a variety of stimulating experiences, each cell is capable of sprouting up to 20,000 different branches to store the new information. In this way, the child literally grows his own brain.

Understanding a child's brain and the way it develops is the key to understanding learning.

Jane M. Healy in
Your Child's Growing Mind

The possible number of connections in the human brain is greater than the number of atoms in the universe.

Robert Ornstein in
The Amazing Brain

LEFT BRAIN - RIGHT BRAIN

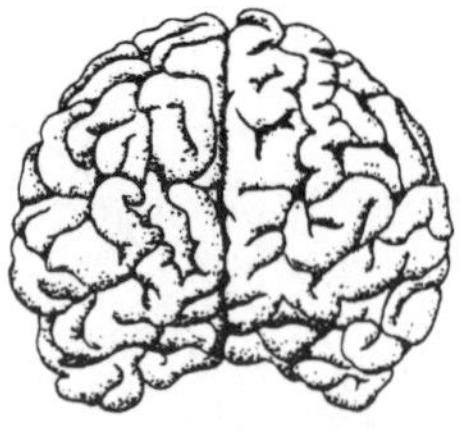

The left side of the brain mainly processes language, logic, mathematics and sequence.

The right side plays a big part in processing music, rhythm, rhyme and artistry.

But children learn fastest when both sides of the brain work effectively together, through a program of overall enrichment.

The brain is really three brains in one. The lower brain deals with instincts like breathing and heartbeat. The middle brain plays a big part in emotion and memory. And the outer brain or cortex folds around the rest like a thin crumpled blanket. It is that outer layer that makes us truly human. It provides us with the ability to speak, read, write, sing, dance, run, play sports, think, reason, and create great masterpieces.

But the emotional middle center of the brain is also vital. It acts as the filter for all information coming into the brain. If a child is under stress or feels threatened, the middle brain will often block information entering the thinking brain. That's why we place so much emphasis on a close, loving bond between parent and child and the need to make learning fun and not forced.

The brain also has two distinct sides. The left side plays a big part in processing logic, reason and language: the so-called academic abilities. The right side plays a key part in processing music, rhyme and rhythm: the so-called creative activities. In fact, the brain works best — and everyone learns more effectively — when both sides work smoothly together.

The reason that it is relatively easy to learn the words of popular songs is because the right brain is processing the music while the left brain is processing the words. And, of course, the emotional center of the brain is also involved.

Enabling your children to develop all that 'brain power' is at the core of the *FUNdamentals* program. The good news: it can all be done easily, with fun, common sense and enjoyment.

Your child's seven intelligences, waiting to be developed

Professor Howard Gardner, of Harvard University, has shown through ground-breaking research that each person's brain has at least seven different intelligences.

They are linguistic, logical-mathematical, musical, visual-spatial, bodily-physical, interpersonal (or social), and intrapersonal (or introspective) intelligence.

Some people may be better at some things than others. But everyone can develop all these intelligences to a much greater degree.

One of the keys to raising a happy, healthy, self-confident child is to encourage a variety of activities which continually stimulate each of the intelligence centers of the brain.

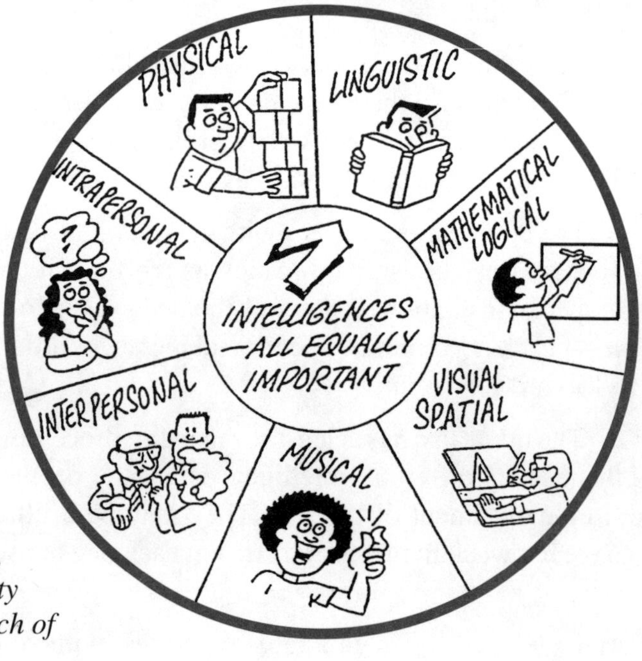

2. Learning through all the senses

There are five main pathways into your baby's brain.

From his very first days he develops the parts of his brain that deal with what he sees, hears, touches, tastes and smells. The more he can see, hear, feel, taste and smell new experiences, the easier and more efficiently he will learn.

From late in the first year of life, the child also makes amazing developments in his *motor* ability—his ability to crawl, walk, climb, dance, run, somersault, turn, twist, skip and spin. This enables him to explore by doing.

And when he can see, hear, touch, taste, smell AND DO things at the same time, he learns at a remarkable rate.

All these activities help create a *feedback learning loop:* the more he *does* the more he learns.

Ultimately, he learns to walk by walking. He learns to talk by listening and talking. He learns to climb by climbing. To ride a tricycle, and then a bike, by riding. To sing, by singing. To write, by writing.

In the first years of life a child has a truly absorbent mind. He soaks up experiences.

He loves to experiment, to create, to explore, to find out how things work. The more his parents or parent can aid that exploration process, the more effectively he will lay down the patterns on which all future learning will be based. Apart from the vital ingredients of love, comfort and food, the most important thing he needs is an environment in which he can 'explode into learning' through all his senses.

In this context, the most effective parents see themselves as mentors and coaches, not as lecturers; as environmental designers, not as teachers. They encourage children to develop their own abilities, to learn by their own achievements—and also their own mistakes. Real knowledge is self-knowledge, the knowledge that comes from self-discovery and multi-sensory exploration.

> *All children are born geniuses, and we spend the first six years of their lives degeniusing them.*
>
> Buckminster Fuller

> *Tell me, I forget. Show me, I remember. Involve me, I understand.*
>
> Old Chinese proverb

> *A child has a built-in drive to explore, to investigate, to try to seek excitement and novelty, to learn by using every one of his senses, to satisfy his boundless curiosity.*
>
> Joan Beck in *How To Raise A Brighter Child*

Fun-filled enthusiasm

> *By the age of five years, parents have taught their children to be virtually independent. It is an incredible achievement.*
>
> Peter Young and Colin Tyre in *Teach Your Child To Read*

If forced to summarize this program in two words, these words would probably be: **have fun.**

Have fun with your children from the moment they are born. Children are natural learners. They have an insatiable desire to find out about everything. They love music, dancing, painting, working with clay, playing games, acting.

They love color, excitement, fantasy, dressing up, make-believe. They learn best whenever they have the opportunity for fun-filled exploration and action—and time for quite reflection. The more you can help create that atmosphere, the greater the experience for both parent and child. Equally: if it's not fun for both parent and child, stop.

The stages of growth

> *All children learn through active participation, by being involved in a practical way, and by attempting to do something themselves, particularly by using their hands.*
>
> Lesley Britton in *Montessori: Play & Learn*

In the first eight years of life, in particular, those discoveries unfold in different stages. Obviously a child learns to crawl before he walks; walks before he runs. In part this is due to the way in which the brain grows and links in sequence with the rest of the body.

And while a child generally finds problems if he 'tries to walk before he can run,' he can speed up any sequence he likes, so long as he has the chance.

Parents should try to understand those stages of growth. But please remember that no child develops at the same pace. Each one is an individual. Einstein was probably the greatest scientist of the 20th century, but he hardly spoke until he was four.

There's also no magic process that enables children to learn without personal experience. A four-year-old, for instance, will only be able to recite a nursery rhyme if he has heard that rhyme several times. A five-year-old will only be able to tie her shoelaces if she has had experience tying laces. It is up to parents to provide the right environment.

> *You should function more as a scene-setter who provides a loving atmosphere full of learning experiences your child can choose for himself, and as a coach who cheers him on and shares the exhilaration of his accomplishments.*
>
> Joan Beck in *How To Raise A Brighter Child*

The more you can provide a rich, stimulating environment for all the senses, the better your child will bloom.

With those provisos, let's get started!

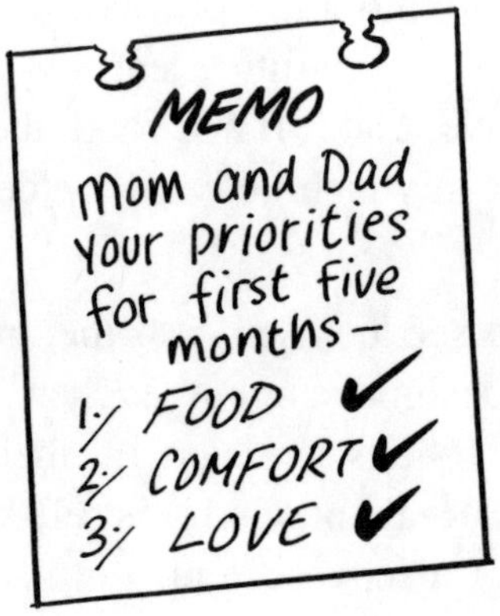

Baby's skin and 'tactile receptors' are more developed at birth than her sight and sound pathways. So plenty of stroking and cuddling, please! You can't spoil a baby with too much attention in the first five months of life.

3. Birth to six weeks

A newborn baby can cry, suck, grasp, and will make occasional glances at nearby objects. These are almost certainly instinctive. The thinking, reasoning brain is not wired up yet. The baby can see to a limited extent and has been able to hear since she was in the womb.

In the first six weeks of life, her main need is for food, comfort and love. Provide lots of all three. When she cries, she almost certainly needs attention. Give it to her. A loving, caring relationship between mother and baby, in particular, is the first step towards the making of a happy, contented child.

Almost every other animal can walk almost immediately after birth, and run soon afterwards. Only humans spend their first few months completely dependent on someone else.

Mothers instinctively rock their babies, probably without realizing that it promotes brain growth!

Developing the senses

Many simple physical activities early in life can help build important 'academic' activities. Scientists have proved, for instance, that regularly rocking a baby can help greatly in promoting brain growth. It stimulates what they call the *vestibular system.*

This is the nerve system centered in the cerebellum and brain-stem and linked very closely to a baby's inner-ear mechanism.

It's the way in which the inner-ear and cerebellum develop together that determines coordination and balance. This is the mechanism that will be needed later for walking, running and riding a bicycle.

Infants who are given periodic vestibular stimulation — by simply rocking — gain weight faster, develop vision and hearing earlier and demonstrate distinct sleep cycles at a younger age. It's been shown that even 15 minutes of rocking, rubbing, rolling and stroking a premature baby four times a day will help her greatly to coordinate movements and ability to learn.

If baby has been fed, burped and is still crying, often rocking is all that is required to calm her down. If she is still crying, try the 'elevator move.'

Hold baby facing you, firmly against your upper body. Then try and duplicate the effect you experience when you are in an elevator and it stops abruptly (but not too abruptly). Do this, simply by bending your knees, five or 10 times. As well as lulling baby into a relaxed state it provides more vestibular stimulation.

Gradually, from around four weeks of age, babies begin to show more interest in their surroundings. But visually, that is generally restricted to very close range. In fact, their best focusing area seems to be about five to 18 inches from the eyes (about 13 to 45 cm).

A baby is born into a world in which, essentially, he is blind, can't hear very well and his sensation is far from perfect. And that's a very uncomfortable place for a baby to be. He's trying to figure out: 'Where am I? What's going on? What's going to happen next?' That's because he can't see, he can't hear and he can't feel very well.

So I think the job of a parent is very clear: to give enough visual, auditory and tactile stimulation so that the baby can get out of this dilemma of not being able to see, hear or feel.

Janet Doman, director of the Institutes for the Achievement of Human Potential in Philadelphia

Use these bold visual stimulators from birth

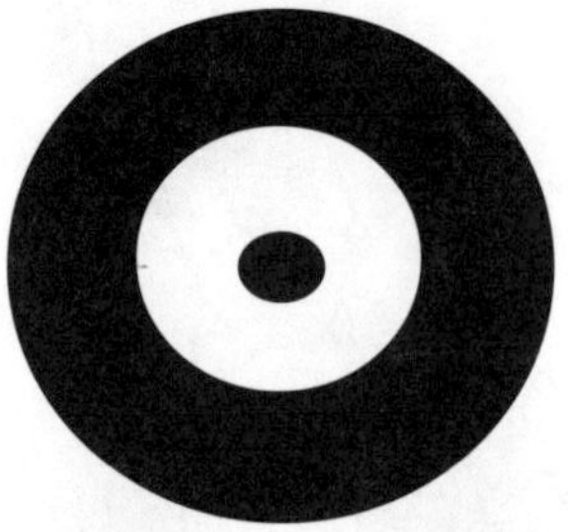

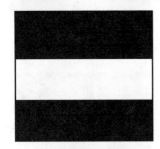

Hang patterned cards such as those illustrated above on your baby's crib with the boldest designs near him. Vary them from day to day. When playing with baby, take one of the bold designs, hold it a few inches from his eyes, and tell him what it is.

At this stage baby needs plenty of strong visual contrasts. That's why we have produced a set of 16 bold black-and-white patterns as a companion to the *First FUNdamentals* program. It's important that these should hang around his crib or sleeping area so he can see vertical and horizontal stripes, circles, squares and the shape of a face.

Visual stimulation can also be helped by making a black-and-white patterned blanket, instead of the traditional white or pastel bed covers.

We strongly recommend against a bland pastel environment. Bold contrasts are much better to 'wire up' the visual pathways in the brain. In fact, we recommend that you go beyond patterned cards and black-and-white blankets and even 'checker-board' one wall of baby's bedroom with big black and white squares of posterboard. It really helps to turn on baby's vision.

The first six weeks of life and particularly the first three weeks, however, are not the time for too much multi-sensory stimulation at the same time. It's great to handle baby and cuddle him gently, but remember that in the early days he is still recovering from an often rough journey out of the womb and into a starkly contrasting environment.

One sense at a time

Try to cultivate baby's interest with a series of uncomplicated activities that appeal to one sense at a time:

▲ Gentle, soothing music can be played softly in the background, perhaps three times a day: in the morning after the baby has been bathed; as you are feeding him during the afternoon; and at night when he is going to bed. (Ideal music at this tender age is *Peer Gynt Suite*, by Greig; *The Swan*, from *Carnival of the Animals*, by Saint-Saens; and *The Four Seasons*, by Vivaldi.)

▲ Playing music for your baby from the very beginning not only lays down a variety of musical pathways in the brain, it helps develop rhythmic coordination. And that, in turn, subsequently helps develop the ability to read and write.

▲ A minute or two of skin-to-skin stroking, from the back of the head and down the body.

▲ A visual game, such as showing him one of the black-and-white patterned cards.

▲ Rocking gently, to add to the vestibular stimulation. A comfortable rocking chair is recommended from birth. Rhythmic rocking is one of the best forms of early stimulation.

▲ A smelling game, with some pleasant spices, perfumes and herbs, but nothing harsh or too pungent at first.

▲ After three weeks, a tasting game: dipping a cotton swab in orange juice, or some other taste variety and placing it on baby's tongue, telling her what she is tasting.

▲ Try covering a flashlight with colored cellophane and move it from side to side so baby can follow it. But remember—only stimulate one sense at a time.

▲ The tactile — touching, feeling — sense is particularly important in the first year. And a tactile toy can be a great help. You can easily make one yourself: stuff a large clean sock and sew different textures to the outside: corduroy, silk, toweling, velvet, satin, or denim. Add black-and-white eyes and some colored wool for hair—but don't attach buttons or similar objects which baby might try to eat.

Different parts of the brain control different parts of the body. And the more movement and touching experience a youngster gets in the first few years of life, the more thorough the base for later all-round education. For the *kinesthetic* and *tactile* experiences actually grow new branches on the billions of active cells that make up the human brain.

Let baby cuddle her tactile toy often to feel the rich and varied textures. Tell her the name of each one.

You can make a snake or caterpillar the same way. Don't be surprised if this becomes a favorite friend.

Specific movement patterns 'wire up' the whole brain. For example, specific walking, running and clapping exercises lead to coordinated counting and that in turn leads to arithmetic.

Never too young to exercise

Simple exercise routines are also important: help her to 'ride a bicycle' by exercising her legs while she is lying on her back. And exercise her arms in the same way. All of this helps baby to become aware of the different parts of her body and what they are capable of doing—and is good training for the actions that will lead to effective crawling.

If you have access to a warm swimming pool, consider using it: you and your baby together. Some mothers do it almost from birth onwards, in groups with other mothers. Aquarobics — water exercises to music — are recommended for prebirth preparation and sometimes the same facilities can be used after birth.

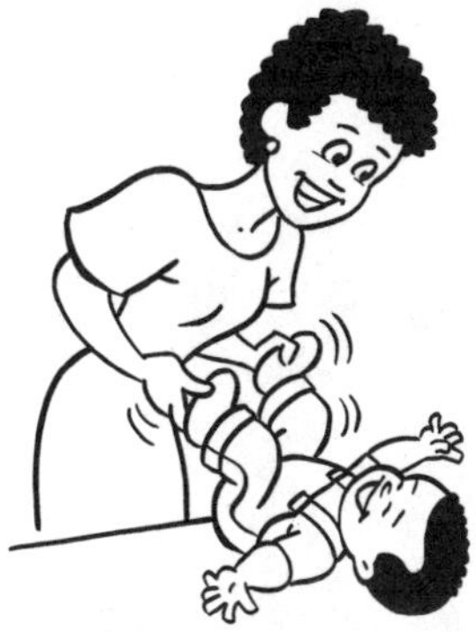

From a few weeks of age your baby will enjoy gentle exercise. Start by helping her 'ride a bicycle' by exercising her legs while she is on her back. Exercise her arms in the same way. Like so many other physical activities, this lays down the 'muscle memory' through which so much other learning takes place.

From as early as two weeks, it is also safe to hold the baby under the arms and encourage her to 'walk,' preferably on bare feet on a firm, flat surface in a warm room. The movement is called reflex stepping and it is particularly strong between two and eight weeks of age.

In one experiment, youngsters who were tested doing reflex stepping began to walk at a much earlier age. Five out of six were walking at 10 months. There is no evidence that such early walking develops more 'intelligence,' but there is no doubt that the sooner children can crawl and walk, the sooner they can explore and learn, and this reduces frustration.

Building a rich vocabulary

The ability to speak fluently is one of the first keys to a flying start in life. So talk to your baby from his earliest days. He won't be able to talk for several months, but he will be able to hear! The more language he hears, the better he will be able to reproduce it later.

Try to look into her eyes as you talk. You may then find yourself 'taking turns' with the baby—she waves her arms, you talk; she waves her arms to get you to talk more and so on.

Once your baby is taking turns to 'talk' you can turn it into more of a game. When the baby makes a sound, imitate it in a singing voice and make more entertaining movements for the baby—shake your head, throw your arms up. Your baby will make more sounds to keep you play-acting to amuse her.

The English language has over 550,000 words. Yet about 90 percent of most speech consists of only about 2,000 to 3,000 words. Most children learn to speak those words in their first three years. With a little bit of help, your child could easily speak 4,000 to 5,000 words before starting school. And he could have the keys to unlock thousands more.

There are only 44 basic sounds in the English language. A child will normally be able to pronounce all of them fluently — in his own family or neighborhood dialect — by the age of four.

The sequence of language learning is generally straightforward. It's commonsense to start off with nouns — the naming words — because they label what a child can see. Start your baby on a voyage of discovery about her own body. Move your hand over her body, naming each part as you go. "This is Cathy's stomach. And these are Cathy's arms. These are Cathy's fingers. And this is Cathy's thumb."

Nouns are easy because they're 'concrete;' she can see them and touch them. And that's one of the keys to early learning: 'experience, then label.' For instance, the more she can see, touch and taste milk, and hear that it is called 'milk,' the easier it will be for her to unlock the secrets of speech. So talk about the specific things she can touch: "This is Anne's bottle. This is Anne's ball. These are Anne's booties. And this is Anne's Daddy."

All children are linguistic geniuses —witness their ability to learn to speak English in the first three years of life. If they live in a bi-lingual house, they learn two. And if they live in a tri-lingual household, they learn to speak three.

Glenn Doman, founder of the Institutes for the Achievement of Human Potential

Next come the verbs, the action words of the language. Feel free to introduce verbs at the same time, especially where you can demonstrate action. "OK, now drink your milk." "Let's turn you on your back so we can change you." "Now we'll put you in your bath." Verbs will obviously have much more meaning later as soon as your child can walk.

Next—adjectives: Introduce first the simple adjectives that again can be demonstrated, such as colors and sizes. "My, that's a big red ball. And that's a little yellow ball." "Look at that big clock. It's much bigger than my little watch, but they both tell the time."

AND FIVE TOES ON THIS FOOT TOO

Get into the habit of talking about what is happening right here and now. In fact, for the entire first two years, a good guide is to talk specifically only about what is happening to the baby right then.

"This is your bath. And this is nice warm water in the bath. And now I'm putting you in the bath water. Now Kevin's having his bath."

"This is a mirror, and you can see yourself." "I'm your Mommy, and this is your Daddy."

This is because babies cannot understand references to objects that are not present or events that are even half a day into the future—even as late as two years of age.

Colorful, brightly illustrated, simple story books should be part of baby's home environment right from day one. Show her the books, encourage her to focus her eyes on the pictures and tell her what she sees on each page. "This is a house. It's made out of brick and it has a red roof. We live in a house, too." Get her used to the idea that books are fun.

The most important thing about reading to babies when they are young is to associate reading with:

- ▲ being held and cuddled
- ▲ warmth and security
- ▲ your undivided attention
- ▲ the fun of words, rhymes and pictures
- ▲ feeling and exploring things beyond their own home.

Swimming in a warm pool is recommended almost from birth. It's great for stimulating brain-building movement, and it also encourages mother-baby bonding.

HEALTH ALERT

If a child has undetected severe ear infection in the first few years of his life this will generally show up in an inability to speak.

In many countries up to a quarter of all infants suffer from a complaint known as glue ear, or otitis media, in one ear. Up to 10 percent have it in both ears.

Glue ear occurs when the Eustachian tube, which connects the back of the nose to the middle ear, becomes blocked. The middle ear fills with fluid and that interferes with the normal vibrations of the ear drum. If left untreated, the fluid turns into a sticky composition like glue. If not removed, it can lead to severe hearing loss and learning difficulties.

TO CHECK YOUR CHILD'S HEARING

In the first three months, clap sharply from three to six feet away.

From 3 to 10 months, baby should turn his head in the direction of any sound, such as the telephone ringing, the sound of people talking.

From 10 to 15 months, the child should start to imitate simple words and sounds.

If this doesn't happen, take your child to a doctor or a hearing clinic for a more thorough check.

Hearing loss is the biggest single cause of speech problems.

So regular hearing checks are a top priority for encouraging a child to speak fluently.

4. Six weeks to six months

From six weeks switch to narrower visual stimulators

After six weeks, use 'visual stimulator' cards with smaller circles, stripes and squares.

N.B. Use them in the car, too.

Your child's 'visual brain' has five separate layers, and each one 'translates' different shapes. So the more contrasting shapes a baby sees, the better her visual discrimination is developed.

Amazingly, if baby saw only horizontal lines in her first few months of life, and no vertical lines, she would later not be able to 'see' the legs of a chair or table.

From six weeks to six months, most babies develop at a fantastic rate, even though they can't yet talk, crawl or walk.

During this exciting period your baby's visual capabilities will improve dramatically. He will begin to 'babble' and make sounds that will eventually become real words. He'll probably become able to roll from his stomach on to his back and by month six from his back on to his stomach. He'll love splashing in the bath and playing peek-a-boo.

And in general he'll begin to show some real interest in the world around him.

Developing the senses

By six weeks, start using bold black-and-white cards with smaller circles, stripes and squares, so baby can see more detailed contrasts. Baby will also — about this time — begin using her hands to 'bat' or swipe at anything around. So make or buy a contrasting stable mobile that baby can both see and hit with her hands.

Between six weeks and six months, consider a simple crib gym, with solid items that baby can bat, touch and grasp. All will develop brain pathways that will later play a key part in reading and writing.

Kick toys, such as a large soft ball placed at the bottom of the crib, are also great so she can exercise her feet and leg muscles, getting ready for crawling and walking.

By six weeks, she should also be starting to gain head control. So place her on her stomach when she's awake and talk to her, from close by and up to 10 feet away. It will help develop neck muscles, eyesight and hearing.

By two months, you can stimulate the auditory system by investing in some wrist rattles, which attach to the wrist by Velcro.

As early as you like and up to three months, consider propping her up in an infant seat, again so she can see more and develop her head control. Make sure the seat is well made and stable.

By three and a half months most babies have almost full visual capacities. You can help this growth by providing plenty of visual stimulation. Your child will spend a lot of time in her bedroom or nursery. So make it interesting.

▲ If you've checkerboarded a wall add brightly colored shapes to the center of each square: circles, triangles, squares, ovals, rectangles.

▲ Try moving her crib around the room, so she can see different sights—some days let her see the world outside; some days move the mirror; other days rearrange the bright posters around the walls.

▲ What can she see on the ceiling, or up high? A plain white ceiling is certainly not the most interesting sight, so hang mobiles, paper kites, colored streamers.

▲ Use flowers, plants, colorful bottles and wind chimes to stimulate the senses. The wind chimes are useful for developing musical and listening skills. You can buy them cheaply or you can make them yourself by hanging different length spoons from a length of wooden dowel. Change the decorations regularly!

▲ Explore nature together at every opportunity. And make 'quiet time' available too, in gardens, parks and fields. Talk to baby about what you can both see: the beauty of nature in the clouds, trees, flowers and rivers.

Between 14 weeks and six months, she'll gradually start to improve her hand-eye coordination, especially if she has well-designed crib toys.

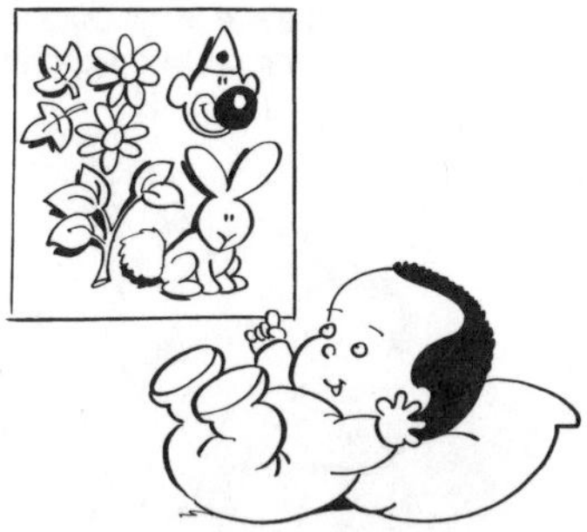

Make your own textured wall pictures. Cut out shapes of animals, flowers and clowns. Add painted ping-pong balls for noses; fabric ears for animals.

Building a rich vocabulary

Children start to 'babble' between three and six months of age. Some linguistic experts say that, during this time, they make all the sounds that occur in any language in the world.

And most educational psychologists agree that babies born in one country, will, over their first year of life, also make sounds heard only in languages from other countries, even if they have never heard these sounds.

If the child lives in a house where two languages are spoken, he will almost certainly learn both. And if three languages are spoken, he will learn three.

Remember there are thought to be about 44 sounds in the English language and only about 70 in all the languages of the world. Again, if a child is exposed to all of them early in life, chances are he will be able to pronounce them properly if he ever has to learn a particular language later.

From two months of age, baby becomes fascinated with his own hands. So invest in some wrist rattles, attached to a wrist with Velcro. The rattle sound helps develop his auditory pathways for better hearing. And, as he tracks the sound of the rattle, he improves his eye-hand coordination, which is essential later for crawling, walking, reading and writing.

Just as the brain starts to open up all its major pathways for learning in the first four years of life, this seems doubly important in the case of speaking.

From the age of about four months as baby starts to make utterances, repeat his sounds back to him. This way of communicating encourages him to keep vocalizing. Try increasing the number of repetitions to see if he copies you. It's best to repeat back a single sound (e.g. 'la, la' or 'da, da'), but do vary the pitch or tempo of the sound to keep your baby interested. It's these bits of sound that will later make up words.

Tape record him and play his voice back to him. As you replay your baby's sounds, e.g. 'buh,' 'muh,' 'ee,' place his fingers on your lips. Let him feel the vibrations as each sound is made. Tape record Mommy and Daddy's voice, too, and watch his reactions when the sound comes from the tape player and not you.

Put a mirror — about the same size as the face — in the crib on the opposite side of the baby to the black-and-white visual stimulation cards.

The brain stores information like branches on a tree. So when you see a new subject — a bird, a dog, a horse, a tree or a flower — try to build on your

THESE ARE YOUR EYES AND THEY'RE BLUE!

Well before baby can speak, he can understand what you are saying. This is because the hearing and visual pathways to his brain are already well insulated, but his speech pathways are not. So talk to him often about what he can see and touch, starting with his own body.

THAT'S A JUICY RED APPLE, AND THAT'S A BIG BLUE BALL

Start with books that have simple clear objects you can describe and relate to real life.

child's existing knowledge. But keep it conversational. "These are some more birds. We call them seagulls. And those birds over there are sparrows."

In this way, your child builds up the bird file in her brain, and all future brain information will be linked to that base. **The more she links the more she learns.** That's not only the key to storing information; it's probably the biggest key to remembering it later.

Regular interaction is vital, even before she can talk.

One British research study showed that active parents at home were averaging 27 conversations an hour with their pre-schoolers: during everyday activities of meals, cooking, cleaning, washing, playing and shopping. Each was feeding the child's insatiable curiosity.

But when the researchers checked the same children after a year at nursery school, teachers were averaging only 10 conversations an hour. It is just impossible for even a brilliant teacher with a class of 10 to 30 children to equal the one-to-one interaction of parent and child.

By four months, invest in some thick-card books with strong, bold simple pictures. The benefits are four-fold: the books are hinged, and that is good for baby's motor development; they're good for 'gumming' in the period before teething; they introduce words and pictures and the whole concept of reading; and looking at them together enables parent and child to bond.

Nursery rhymes: The reason nursery rhymes endure is that the repetition of the same words and rhythm over and over again helps babies realize that certain sounds have meanings. Rhymes and songs that combine action are especially helpful because they give clues to meaning: e.g. "pat-a-cake, pat-a-cake, baker's man."

Give a simple running commentary on the everyday things you and your baby do and see—continue to stress the key words and names.

When you see your baby looking at something, name it and, if possible, give it to him to handle.

Name people for him as they appear and use your own name as you do things for your baby, e.g. "Mommy's going to change you now."

Developing music and listening skills

Vary your voice tone. Make a conscious effort sometimes to vary from a high to a low pitch; from soft to enthusiastic. It maintains your baby's interest as you talk to her. Whispering into your baby's ear occasionally also builds interest and is calming. It also encourages her to listen more closely.

Call baby's name softly before she sees you enter a room and give her time to locate you. It helps her become alert to language. When she sees you, give her a big hug of encouragement.

5. Six months to twelve months

By six months, baby should be able to see and hear extremely well. By seven months most children can sit unaided. And before long they're crawling, becoming much more inquisitive and getting into all kinds of mischief.

By the end of his first year he'll be playing with manipulative toys, will be able to understand simple commands, say a few words and start showing moods and emotions.

AND NOW FOR ANOTHER MAGIC SMELL

Mom can turn herself into a "playmobile" with a smock-full of simple toys and effects (see activity card #28.)

Developing the senses

As you talk to your baby, nod occasionally up and down. See if she follows your actions. If she waits until you've stopped, she is beginning to adjust how she behaves to fit your actions.

All babies like dropping things from their high chair. Here's a game which shows them that what goes down can be pulled back up—and lets them do the pulling. Tie a light toy onto a piece of yarn and attach it to the high chair. Pulling it up is a more difficult skill than dropping it, but your baby will be delighted at the accomplishment.

Another pulling game: position a blanket so the edge is within easy reach of your seated baby. Place a favorite toy on the blanket—out of your baby's reach. Wait a moment and see if he can work out how to get the toy. Show him how by tugging on the blanket yourself, if necessary.

And a pushover game: stack plastic tumblers or bricks in front of your child. Let her knock them down (show her how if you have to). She'll enjoy it all the more if you say 'crash' as they tumble down. These games help baby learn how to control arm and hand movements.

Adults know that to point your finger invites the other person to look away in a certain direction. Babies don't! They are quite likely to look at the end of your finger. So — at about the age of eight months — as you teach him what pointing signifies, use your whole arm in an exaggerated gesture—as if you were throwing.

Start by pointing at something nearby. Choose something which he's already looking at which you can also touch, e.g. "There's your cup." Make sure his eyes follow your gesture. As he understands 'pointing' you can then interact better with books and also share things that are further away.

By seven or eight months, most babies will be able to crawl. Some will do it even earlier, if they have had plenty of practice on their stomach. About 25 percent will crawl a little later.

As soon as baby can crawl, safety proof the house— and let him loose!

We have never come across an eight-month-old child who is not incredibly curious. We have never known an eight-month-old child who needed to be reinforced to explore the home once she could crawl.

Bear in mind that to have a very strong exploratory drive is of central importance for humans in that, unlike most other animals, humans go through a very long developmental period and come equipped with fewer instincts than other animals have to cope with the world.

Burton L. White

Your home is his greatest educational institution, but only if he can explore it. The kitchen is every crawler and toddler's first kindergarten. So turn it into one. Make a decision. Your baby's development is more important than the neatness of your home or cupboards.

Remove from bottom cupboards and lower pantry shelves everything you don't want touched—especially breakable kitchenware—or install childproof latches. And childproof every area up to two feet from floor level. Make sure to childproof ashtrays, plants, vases, electrical sockets and anything that has inviting holes, such as the cassette slot on a videotape player.

Left to himself he'll be able to experiment with the consequences of his actions, repeat actions that have surprising effects, fit shapes into pots and pans and containers—and imitate you!

Rolling a ball backwards and forwards develops 'big motor' abilities which must be built before fine motor skills like writing.

Babies should be given the chance to crawl from as early an age as possible. They can actually crawl from birth but are usually restricted by so much clothing that they don't develop this ability until later. The more they crawl the sooner they're going to get around holding onto things, and the sooner they're going to be able to walk. And each of these stages ensures that the next stage comes at the right moment—and they have completed the neurological maturation that goes with it.

Crawling is a vital stage of development in which baby is 'forced' to develop the ability to converge his two roving eyes—so he doesn't bump into everything!

When your baby wakens up after a sleep, go to him with your arms held out. Pause for a few seconds before you pick him up and give your baby time to reach out or push himself towards you. He'll find some way of letting you know he wants picking up. Pick him up and cuddle and play with him.

Don't let him become frustrated or angry—just wait long enough to give him the chance to 'tell' you what he needs.

Independent learners can say what they think. Early experiences of telling others what he needs, and having his needs met as a consequence, helps him become a person who can let others know what he is thinking.

For crawling a baby needs to use all four limbs in that cross-patterning sequence that is one of the key essentials of total human development. The movement strengthens the pathways that link both sides of the brain. The importance of 'cross-patterning' cannot be emphasized enough.

You can help baby to crawl by putting a favorite toy just out of reach and encouraging her to move to get it. If she makes a determined effort but can't quite reach the toy make a game out of bouncing or rolling it towards her.

In many ways, crawling enables each baby to turn a big developmental corner. He starts to focus on the world of small objects. And he starts to learn about cause and effect as he explores shapes, forms, textures—everything. It is only by exploring a great variety of objects, with all one's senses, that the foundation for later knowledge is laid.

One of the best objects of all is a big ball. Sit your child on the floor with legs apart and roll the ball between his legs, encouraging him to roll it back to you. It may take a few tries for him to get the idea, but persevere and make it a fun game. This helps baby develop big muscle or 'big motor' abilities which are essential before he can handle more intricate maneuvers such as writing.

If crawling is the first step on that discovery process, climbing is generally the second—usually by about 11 or 12 months. Then around that time, he also starts to walk; sometimes sooner, sometimes later. He will first learn to pull himself up and start 'cruising'—walking around holding on to other objects. He will start pulling himself up stairs and then taking the first tentative steps by himself.

Now's the time to introduce the first manipulative toys such as stacking blocks and big pegboards. Not only do these develop the muscular skills for later writing and painting, they also encourage him to experiment with fitting shapes together which is one of the core concepts of creative art.

A pegboard with large round pegs is a great gift for baby's first birthday. Being able to place the pegs properly is another important developmental milestone: also vital for hand-eye coordination. Most children will be able to do this between 12 and 18 months but don't try and force the pace. Simply provide the opportunity.

Around 12 months of age, provide your child with a big peg board. Playing with this develops finger control, and hand-eye coordination, that will later be important for good writing.

By his first birthday, too, he can generally jabber a few single words and he can certainly understand a lot more. He can usually wave goodbye, respond to his own name, eat finger food, remove the lid of a box to retrieve an object, build a tower of two or three blocks.

And if by then he can take only a few steps unaided, generally within two months he's up and running.

By now you can also teach baby to understand and recognize that images represent real things by playing the "Where's Grandma?" game. Place two family photos side-by-side, for example of a brother, or Dad or Grandma or someone else she sees every day. Ask her to find one, perhaps Grandma first, and then Dad. Later on try covering up both with a piece of paper or booklet and ask her again.

'Mirror Games' are a great way to help baby realize that things can be out of sight but still exist. Cover a mirror with a cloth and sit in front of it with your baby on your lap. Then uncover it and say: "Look there is Jenny."

She'll probably be surprised at seeing herself and discovering that you can be holding her and be in the mirror at the same time. Play covering and lifting a few times. You can also use the mirror game to show the baby her mouth and nose and ears, which otherwise are more difficult for her to understand, and to experiment with different faces. Try putting on a different hat or a blob of lipstick on her nose. See if she imitates your expression. She is learning about her body and what it can do.

Whenever you're playing with baby, tell him the names of everything he can see, starting with his toys. From about 12 months, encourage him to identify his toys by saying, "Where's the ball?" Give him time to look at it, touch it or pick it up. If he doesn't, then pick it up yourself and say, "Here's the ball," as you give it to him. Learning to label things is the first step to a rich vocabulary.

Building a rich vocabulary

Use names and stress them. Babies learn the meaning of a word by constantly hearing it in different ways but always associated with the same thing (not by repeating single words over and over).

So stress key words in your sentences and use them rather than pronouns (i.e. he, she or it). e.g. "Where's the *cup?* Oh, here's the *cup* (not here it is). Here's some *bread* for *Mommy*. And here's some *bread* for *Catherine*."

Exaggerate! Mime the language so it's, for example, "*high* up in the air" (your hands over your head); "*low* down on the ground" (crouch down).

Simple hand puppets are a great device to encourage conversation. Have your puppet say something, then pause to allow your baby space and time to reply—even if it is only to laugh or touch the puppet. Don't overload him, though, with too much talk from the puppet.

If a small child learns the sound of the word 'nose' as you touch his nose, and he sees the word nose in bold type at the same time, he will soon learn to read and write at the same time. Even very young babies, from around four months, have visual pathways sufficiently developed to be able to see words with letters about 2.5 inches deep (about 6cm).

We've included a sample set of noun cards with this program. Attach them to items around the home, or show the names of your baby's parts as you talk to her about her eyes, nose and ears. You'll find a full set of 78 nouns and verbs in our FUNdamentals program for toddlers and infants.

When you are reading to your baby, let her turn over the pages so she feels more control. Give her a chance to finish some sentences for you. Prompt her by saying, "That's a big dog. It's a labrador. It says . . ."

Approaching 12 months is the time you can also begin to play the label game—putting big written labels on things your child can see. We've included some examples with your *First FUNdamentals* program. The typeface, style and size have been carefully selected so they can be 'read' by your baby.

nose

ball

cat

Daddy

hand

milk

toes

Nearly all parents expose their infants to speech without thinking about it. But most do not expose them to written words because they think reading is more 'advanced' than speaking. It isn't, because when a child hears the word 'Daddy' she has to interpret the pattern of sound to understand it represents her father. When she sees the word 'Daddy' she has to interpret the **visual** pattern. The process is essentially similar as long as the type size is big enough for the very young eyes to see. That's why we've included some word cards to get you started. But don't introduce all the words at once. Turn it into a game. "This is your nose, and the word says 'nose.' This is your hand, and this word says 'hand.' What a clever girl. You can read 'hand.'"

Some parents label most things a child can see. So if you want to make your own extra cards you can use our set as models. Note that the typeface includes the letters a and g in the same style that your child will later print—not the typographer's style that you are reading now.

Other parents prefer to introduce related words together. So when they are talking about parts of the body they show the word cards for *hand, eyes, hair, nose* and the rest. Still others prefer to write additional words on a whiteboard or blackboard, near their kitchen table or in the nursery.

Again, if you decide to do that, still write them boldly, and in non-capital letters, except for 'proper' names such as *Bobby, Joe* and *Sally.*

Developing music and listening skills

Dance with your baby—from as early as six months! Babies love to be whirled gently around as you dance to music that has a clear rhythm, such as a waltz.

Help baby become familiar with rhythm by tapping out a simple beat while your baby is sitting on your lap. After a while, change to another simple rhythm.

Emotional development

In the vital time from crawling until about 14 months of age most infants have three main interests:

- ▲ Trying to interact with other people—the social interest.
- ▲ Improving or enjoying newly-developing physical skills—the motor interest.
- ▲ And exploring—satisfying curiosity.

How you and she balance those interests in this period will play a key part in shaping her personality.

She'll have to learn to take mishaps in her stride, not gain attention by crying or whining and to avoid other bad habits such as biting and hair-pulling. In many ways, the period from about eight or nine months to three years of age is the major period of socialization. As children develop the power of speech and walking, they move into the world of other people.

During that period they must learn how to ask for help, how to get on with other people, how to handle things they are not supposed to do. They can learn to do those things in a reasonable, pleasant social way. Or they can learn to scream, cry and whine for attention.

Key point for parents: don't reinforce bad behavior, reinforce good

Between the ages of six months and 12 months is a good time to introduce baby to the concept of meeting other people—and to help her be comfortable in doing so.

When you meet a stranger hold your baby secure in your arms. Suggest the person hand her something before touching her. Then when baby is ready to go to the new person, try to busy yourself with something else so she has a chance to explore the person without reference to you.

Pull along games let children explore cause and effect. You can start by pulling the toy and encouraging him to catch it. Make a big fuss when he does. Then swop roles.

Let him experiment with different toys on different surfaces—a yogurt pot, a soft toy, a tin can or a cotton reel on a string pulled along on carpets, grass and gravel. Let him play by himself to see what happens. A stick dragged in the earth, for example, behaves very differently from a balloon dragged along the same surface.

Experiments like these develop an attitude of independence and curiosity.

Babies at around 12 months like books that depict daily routines—visits to shops, meal times, bedtimes, etc. They allow you to build vocabulary on familiar scenes.

6. Twelve months to eighteen months

An infant's next year is quite possibly the most important in his life. This is the time when your child moves into his first period of full exploration. It's the time when he can actually walk and later run to explore his environment, when he learns to talk and communicate, and when he can interact with other people to develop his social skills.

Developing the senses

Peek-a-boo games create delight and understanding that things exist even when you can't see them.

Play hide-and-seek or peek-a-boo with your one-year-old and he'll make amazing strides in improving his memory. For the first time he learns that other objects are permanent, even though he can't see them. That leads to a startling conclusion—he, too, is an independent individual, and his mother and father exist even when he can't see them.

He learns that other people and things also exist in their own right and he can now start to remember them, even when he can't see them. It is the start of memory growth: what the experts call the discovery of 'object permanence.'

Babies love to imitate—that's what they do for a living! So play impromptu copycat games using just hands. For example, you might tap the table, point to your nose, put a hat on your head, wiggle your fingers. Always describe what you're doing as you do it.

From around 12 months most infants can hold a crayon in their fist and start scribbling. Encourage them. By 15 months most children can scribble up and down, by 18 months from left to right, and by 21 months round and round.

Invest in child-sized kitchen and cleaning equipment. Children like to imitate and use their own real, but smaller, brooms, floor mops, dustpans, dusting brushes, cleaning brushes, watering cans, dishcloths, sponges, baskets and small plastic buckets. Real articles are much better than expensive toys.

To keep a lamp burning you have to put oil in it.

Mother Teresa

As she touches and plays with things build up her ability to tell the difference between textures by drawing her attention to different textures: sandpaper is rough, glass is smooth, tissue is soft, fur is very soft, wood is hard, etc.

Shine a flashlight around a darkened room to encourage him to follow it with his eyes. Good for eye-tracking.

Bath time can be the perfect time to expose baby — in a playful way — to a wide variety of important concepts. Try some of these quick games with a purpose:

- ▲ Wrap up a bathtub toy in a washcloth and let him unwrap it.
- ▲ Catch floating toys in a soup ladle or serving spoon.

▲ Blow through a straw into water.

▲ Good bathtub toys are plastic spoons, yogurt containers, bowls, plastic measuring cups, transparent plastic bottles—all of which you can use to talk about 'half full,' ' full,' ' empty,' 'pour,' 'float,' 'measure,' etc. A lot of mathematical discoveries lead from water play.

▲ Listen to different water sounds—dripping, running, spilling, stirring, bubbling.

Building a rich vocabulary

By his first birthday introduce your baby to simple alphabet books, such as *Dr. Seuss's ABC*.

Choose books with simple, clear pictures of everyday objects. Sit with him on your knee, open a book, and wait for the baby to touch a picture. Then point to the same picture and tell him the object's name and some interesting points about it. Then when you see the object in real life, point it out, so he learns that books and information can symbolize reality.

Between one and two, you can introduce your child to the world of adverbs: the words that often tell how we do things or how we feel—most commonly ending in 'ly': quickly, slowly, sadly, finally and gradually.

Try also to introduce simple prefixes into your everyday speech. "You don't look too happy today. What made you unhappy?" Once a child absorbs the message that unhappy means not happy and uncomfortable means not comfortable, he's grasped the key that 'un' before a word means 'not.'

Then introduce a variety of prepositions: words that show positions — under, over, in, at, about, around, across, through.

Keep those simple concepts in mind and it's easy to turn any experience into a chance to develop your child's speaking ability. But you don't have to turn every day into a literature lesson.

Keep it natural. Keep it simple. Keep it fun.

Talk about relationships naturally—and specifically. "Wow! That's a big car. It's bigger than ours." Make sure to use words such as *longer, shorter, over, under, around, closer, before, after, bigger, smaller, lighter, heavier, more, less.* And use them in context. "I think I'll park down here. It's near McDonalds and it's closer to the bank than the other parking lot."

But instructions are not enough. Experience is vital, so make sure he experiences as much as possible: "This is the *cold* water. Let's put a little *hot* water in it and make it *warmer*. Feel that. Now let's make it *hotter* still."

And don't be worried if your child doesn't talk as quickly as another.

In the first 18 months it's much more important for him to *take in* language. Then, when he is ready to speak, it will re-emerge as a rich vocabulary.

I believe that we shall gradually come to take it for granted that children should learn to read, to turn written words into sounds, to write and to spell at home, as naturally as they now learn to hear and speak.

Felicity Hughes in *Reading and Writing Before School*

You can introduce your one-year-old to verbs and adverbs simply by encouraging her to do things: "Let's see how slowly you can roll over."

Developing music and listening skills

▲ Let baby see you put two types of things into two plastic bottles—things that rattle such as stones, rice or beads; then other things that make only a soft sound—rice paper or cloth. Let her shake the bottles while you talk about one being 'noisy' and the other being 'quiet.'

▲ Let her hear the sounds made as she drops different objects—a pan lid, stone, bit of wood, feather, piece of paper . . .

▲ Talk about sounds as they occur: the clock is ticking; the bird is singing; the telephone bell is ringing; the wind is blowing; the rain is pattering; the cat is mewing; the tap is dripping; the water is splashing.

▲ Talk about sounds as you and she make them: we're clapping, tapping, banging, stamping, smacking our lips, whistling, the water is bubbling, the spoon is scraping.

A child wants to learn. *There is no need to do something to motivate him, such as offer him sweets if he learns his two times tables. With sufficient encouragement from you, his inborn motivation to learn will appear. Left to himself a child will spontaneously choose to do something that interests him.*

Unfortunately some children lose this inborn motivation because their natural curiosity has been frustrated.

Lesley Britton, Director of the London Montessori Center

Encouraging creative play

The ability to create is formed largely in the first few years of life.

These are the years when each child has an insatiable desire to learn through all the senses. The more she can explore with all those senses and the more she can reflect on those experiences, the more she develops the ability to perceive reality in different ways.

All later creativity will be built on early concepts of perception. Like all learning, it is built on the interface between the brain, the senses and muscles.

Here are some activities you can introduce to your one-year-old to stimulate his creative capabilities:

Telephone Talk. For babies, even as young as 12 months, the telephone is one of the very best toys. Use either a toy one or temporarily unplug a real one. Show him how to hold the phone and 'talk' to Daddy or Teddy.

Shopping trips will take longer — but provide more learning — if you sometimes let your toddler pick out some of the items. The combination of physically handling fruits and packets while talking about the contents, colors, textures, weights, etc. builds vocabulary quickly.

Make a swish jar. Take a large plastic jar and partially fill it with water —ideally with some blue food dye added. (Glue the lid tight.) Drop objects in that will float, e.g. a table tennis ball, cotton reel, cork. He'll love to rock it and make the contents bob around.

Building bridges. An important milestone for your baby is to be able to put a ruler across two bricks to build a bridge. Start off by showing him how.

What's wrong? Even children as young as one year develop a sense of the ridiculous. So try putting his sock on his head, or your sweater on your head, saying, "Is this right?" It's the start of logical thinking—and great fun. You'll find he often imitates you and laughs.

Feeding toys. Most children like to feed their dolls or Teddies with cookies. It's a good way to introduce the idea of taking turns. "Now then, Helen, it's Teddy's turn to have a cookie." Use it also as a start point to wash a suitable toy, shampoo it, put it to bed, etc.

Imagination is more important than knowledge.

Albert Einstein

Buzz/boop: The next time baby gives you a prod, look surprised and respond with a sound, such as 'Buzz.' She'll probably try again, so you 'buzz' again. It becomes a game where she discovers cause (the poke) and effect (your noise). After the game has gone on for a few moments try a different noise (and facial expression) for example, 'boop.' The surprise reaction will delight her. End the game with a hug and tell her: "What a clever girl. You made me 'buzz' and 'boop.'"

Emotional development

Thwarting the 'terrible twos': Soon after the first birthday and through two years of age, most infants experiment with power. They test who's boss. And this is very much the time to set limits, to establish the principle of parents' as well as a child's rights.

Every one of us has met children who between the ages of one and three throw tantrums, complain incessantly, hit other children and are constantly demanding attention. For many parents the worst years have become known as the 'terrible twos.' But they needn't be.

Most researchers now believe that the so-called 'terrible twos' occur only when parents overindulge their children in the first two years of life.

Young children must be made to realize that anti-social behavior doesn't work—not by spanking them but by making rules that stick.

Most experts will tell you that the 'terrible twos' are caused by over-indulgence during the first two years of life. The best parenting practices involve love and firmness—when the parents, not the baby, run the home.

There's probably not a parent alive who hasn't agonized at some stage over the narrow dividing line between love and spoiling. The simple but not always easy principle of discipline: set the guidelines firmly and don't argue about them—enforce them. Let her know what is required and insist that she pays the consequences. In her eyes, arguing or explaining gets the kind of attention she's seeking.

If she breaks the rules, make sure she knows that she is choosing the consequences: being confined, for example, to a playpen or a 'time out' in a specific chair.

I honestly believe that with very few exceptions, the common, extremely unpleasant behaviors of those three-year-olds we call "spoiled" were unknowingly taught to them by parents who loved them.

Burton L. White in *Raising A Delightful, Unspoiled Child*

Like everything else an infant does, she learns self-reliance, self-discipline, self-respect, self-perception and a sense of personal values from practice. All are inter-related keys to 'good behavior' and self-identity.

Once again, the key role for parents is to foster a learning environment which encourages children to build their own inner strength, to fashion their own behavior.

After baby's first birthday you can begin to help him understand his own feelings and begin to think about other people's needs. If your child is happily playing with Teddy, try introducing a blanket and bottle. Then say, "What does Teddy need? Is he hungry? Does Teddy need a drink? Is he sleepy?"

Remember that the young child's world is the here and now, a world of concrete objects. But they do need to learn about untouchable ideas like feelings. So build up a vocabulary of 'feelings words.' Incorporate these words into the physical world.

Some examples:-

"Well, Catherine is *excited* to walk so far."

"Helen is *pleased* with those drawings, isn't she?"

"Peter is *happy* with that flower, isn't he?"

"Malcolm is *upset* because he can't open the box."

'Tis easier to prevent bad habits than to break them.

Benjamin Franklin

Words for feelings — including negative feelings — are very important. Later, children who cannot express feelings in words are more likely to resort to physical means—which could include violence. It will be some time before baby understands his feelings but talking about them shows that words help tell what he is feeling.

Dolls and Teddies are invaluable for pretend play that acts out potentially fearful experiences, e.g. having an injection, a visit to the dentist. Also as a later outlet for anger or frustration—for example at the arrival of a new baby.

IT WORKED YESTERDAY, LETS SEE IF I CAN GET HER ATTENTION AGAIN!

Toys are also useful as 'props' when you are making up a story with your child, moving the toys and making the appropriate noises.

Giving and taking: Take every opportunity to share with your child—and show her that giving to others is an important human pleasure.

Offer to let her hide things in your pocket, or put things in your lap. If she offers you a toy, take it and thank her—but give it back quickly. Then she learns that sharing something doesn't mean losing it forever—it's only temporary. This encourages her to share voluntarily.

Help her to see that giving is pleasurable by taking two cookies or oranges. Say: "This is for Susan. This is for Mommy. Would you like to give Mommy her cookie?" She can now give it to Mommy because she still has one left! Make a big fuss when Mommy receives it so she equates giving with pleasure. Keep building on this pattern and she will come to share generously.

One of the hardest, but most important, tasks of young parenthood is to determine what is a genuine cry from hunger or discomfort to a cry solely for attention. As soon as you feel your child is crying only for attention, say something like, "I'm busy preparing dinner right now. I'll come and help you shortly." More detailed advice on behavioral problems is given in our main FUNdamentals *program.*

Taking Turns: You can build on pleasurable giving with a simple game which only needs two toys. Start by saying, "It's your turn to play with the ball. It's not Daddy's turn. Daddy will play with the bricks."

After a while suggest, "Now it's Daddy's turn to play with the ball. Billy had a turn with the ball; now it's Daddy's turn. Billy can play with the bricks," and exchange the bricks for the ball. Smile and hug or pat him and say, "You are so good at taking turns."

It's important to repeat one word like *turn* so as not to confuse him. Make sure you always swap toys immediately so he's not empty-handed! You need to play this game a lot before it's learned. Later, you can remind him to 'take turns' when playing with other children.

7. A word about Reading

Your baby reading some words before his second birthday? Amazingly, it's quite simple. In fact, there is strong evidence that it's at least as easy to read as it is to talk. That's because . . .

▲ The ability to see is developed before the ability to talk.

▲ And a clearly-written word looks the same to whoever sees it, while the same word may be confusing to the ear because it can be spoken in hundreds of different accents and dialects.

At least the producers of television commercials are in no doubt. They present their messages in clear simple written words, graphics and sound. There's probably a rhyming jingle set to music to appeal to other key processing parts of the brain. And, of course, most TV commercials also have an emotional appeal.

When you're first reading to baby, choose books with simple, clear pictures, preferably with only one object on a page. Talk to her about each picture.

So even young babies grow up recognizing McDonalds, Coca Cola and dozens of other brand names. Very simply, these babies have broken the code. They've been able to do it because the wording on television commercials and on advertising billboards is big enough for infants' emerging visual pathways to handle.

Infants only find it hard to read if the print is too small. When they see words written in big type — and those words are related to the infants' own experiences — they learn to read easily.

This is not surprising. For language consists of *symbols* — words — which are communicated by both *sound* and *shape*. ***And it makes no difference to the brain whether it receives those symbols through the ears or the eyes.*** Both provide similar sensory pathways into the brain.

All parents expose their infants to speech without thinking about it. But most do not expose them to written words because that means making or finding special materials.

So as your child is beginning to speak, and much earlier if you like (as discussed in the 'Six months to twelve months' segment), consider introducing word games with bold written labels on cards to reinforce the spoken word. Start with words that mean something specific to your child, such as the parts of his body. Then use similar cards to label items in the nursery, kitchen, etc.

Good parents teach reading by interacting with their children in exactly the same way as they teach them so successfully to walk and talk.

Peter Young and Colin Tyre in *Teach Your Child To Read*

▲ Later, play the game with words he wants. Get him to choose one or two words a day. Write each on a card and keep in his own magic box.

▲ Install a whiteboard in the nursery or kitchen. Write a new magic word on it every night, and each morning make a game out of learning it.

▲ Point out the big words that abound outside your home: the names of streets, billboards, signs in supermarkets.

8. A word about Writing

The children who came were from the humblest social levels and their parents were illiterate. Yet these children learned to read and write before they were five and no one had given them any lessons. If visitors asked them, "Who taught you to write?", they often answered with astonishment, "Taught me? No one has taught me!"

Maria Montessori in *The Absorbent Mind*

Learning to write can become almost as easy as learning to read. In fact, some children find it easier.

The reason is probably two-fold: children can ***explode*** into writing, virtually without instruction, if their environment provides them with the choice of equipment and activities to develop *pre-writing* abilities.

Given those early pre-writing experiences, they find writing easier because they are expressing their own thoughts, while in reading they have to understand the thoughts of others.

There are, of course, three aspects of writing:

How you write: the physical ability to use crayons, pencils or pens to print words or write them in a flowing, linked script.

What you write: your ability to put your thoughts on paper.

Getting it right: your ability to spell, punctuate and link sentences so they make sense.

All three skills can be developed naturally. And most children can master the *physical* skills of writing well before they start school. But the keys to unlock this remarkable ability start even before the first birthday.

Puzzles with big knobs are ideal for pre-writing experience, even for infants as young as 12 to 14 months. Choose some early ones with simple pieces: squares, triangles and circles, so your infant can piece them together. Introduce these about the same time as big peg boards, and stacking blocks and cones.

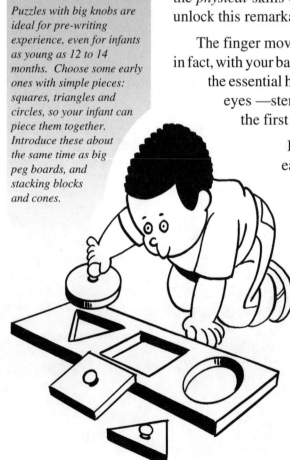

The finger movements that will ultimately lead to writing ability begin, in fact, with your baby's first clutching and grasping movements. Then comes the essential hand-eye coordination skill and the ability to converge the eyes —stemming directly from crawling (on hands and knees) and the first attempts at walking.

Big pegboards are other early landmarks on the way to early writing. So are wooden puzzles with big pieces and big knobs so youngsters around 12 months can start to develop 'big motor' skills with their hands. Also recommended are stacking blocks and cones.

As you sit on the floor and roll a ball back and forth to your baby, you're also developing hand-eye coordination that will later help with painting and writing.

Then between 12 and 18 months introduce large-bead threading, for finer motor skills.

As soon as your child can do this, choose toys or manipulative puzzles that have even smaller knobs so that she can start coordinating fingers and thumbs for later writing ability.

9. A word about Mathematics

Teach this . . .

Four buttons and five ice cream cones represent concrete information about numbers.

. . . before this

4 and 5 are abstract numerals.

Mathematics? In a program for infants?

Yes! But if you still have horrifying memories of high school mathematics, we appreciate that the concept of 'fun-filled' math lessons may be hard to accept. Fact is: basic mathematics concepts *are* simple.

For many of us they became hard because we learned them too late! And because generally we were taught with abstract symbols rather than concrete objects. We now know that that is the wrong way to learn anything.

Everyone learns best from concrete experience. We learn much easier when we first *experience,* then *label.* And that applies even more to small children. Basic to all mathematics is the ability to count. Yet some young children are taught to count without knowing what the numbers mean. They don't understand that the numeral 6, for instance, stands for 'six of something.'

And any child who doesn't appreciate that numbers are based on real things will have a hard task learning arithmetic.

> *A child who knows that numbers represent actual objects has a solid foundation for going on to addition, subtraction, multiplication and division.*
>
> Jean Marzollo and Janice Lloyd in *Learning Through Play*

The counting game

Remember that from the time you start talking to your baby you can turn counting into a game. "These are your eyes. You've got two eyes, but only one mouth and one nose." Count the buttons on his coat, the toys in his crib. But whatever you count, count *something*: peas, money, books, steps, hand claps.

Teach math with all the senses. Get him to: "Take five giant steps. Count them now: one, two, three, four, five! Now see how many times you can hop. One, two . . ." "Now let's see how many buttons we can throw into a box."

From the time your child starts 'helping' in the kitchen you can turn many of your fun-filled activities into mathematics lessons: teaching him to count, measure, subtract and divide.

The one overriding principle applies: every child develops best by involving ALL his senses, and by physically doing.

> *Counting is the seed from which all mathematics sprouts. To help you get along, here's a list of things to count: dishes on the dinner table, spoons in the kitchen drawer, cookies on a plate, stuffed animals on the child's bed, towels in the bathroom, plants in the living room, pencils on the desk, dishes at the dinner table, peanuts in a bowl, ice cubes in a tray.*
>
> Peggy Kaye in *Games For Learning*

10. All you need is love

It's impossible to spoil a young child with too much love.

> *Personally I think love is the most essential ingredient. Warmth and affection is the prime consideration for healthy brain development. But from then on, expose them to a great variety of experiences.*
>
> Prof. Marian Diamond, the researcher who dissected Albert Einstein's brain

That's the most vital ingredient of all: the knowledge that you're loved by the person you love most. The need to feel secure and safe is basic to any child's development. And on that base you can build a pyramid of common sense:

No put-downs, only put-ups. Positive praise for tasks attempted; positive encouragement to tackle more.

A child is not his actions. There's a world of difference between, "You're a bad, naughty boy," and, "I love you, but I don't like what you did."

Model self-respect. In so many ways, a child's parents are his mirror. An infant's language, self-respect and confidence are modeled more on her parents than anyone else.

Model positive attitudes. Most tasks in life can be viewed as problems or opportunities. As challenges or curses. And again your own attitudes provide the model. For a start, try smiling every time something goes wrong. You'll be amazed how quickly it then comes right.

> *We learn to love by being loved unconditionally.*
>
> Linda and Richard Eyre in *Teaching Your Children Values*

It is sheer joy to help frame the environment in which children flower: where they learn to talk, walk, read, write, draw, create, solve problems, set values, make decisions. But the greatest gift of all is love.

In *First FUNdamentals* we have distilled the best information from around the world to guide new parents on this remarkable journey but it's important not to lose sight of the most fundamental lesson of all.

It's summed up neatly in this quote:

> "All the wisdom in the world cannot, by itself, replace intimate human ties, family ties, as the center of human development."
>
> Selma H. Fraiberg in *The Magic Years*

> *Don't just tell your child you love him —show him.*
>
> Coley Lamprecht in *Every Child a Winner*

11. A word about eating right

"Yes, you are what you eat!" So any program aimed at stimulating a child's mental development would be somewhat lacking if it did not address, at least briefly, the critical issue of proper nutrition.

Human milk is the food of choice for infants.

The Surgeon General's Report on Nutrition and Health

Every mother-to-be knows how vital it is to eat right, i.e. 'while eating for two.' Attention to good dietary habits is just as important *after* birth because 'myelination' (the 'wiring up') of the central nervous system continues until about three years of age. This process requires essential fats, protein and zinc.

The best source of all three is mother's milk, which also contains a wealth of specific protective antibodies which coat the baby's intestines and respiratory tract and fight off infection. It also helps protect from ear infections, various allergies and provides calcium and phosphorus for rapidly growing bones.

In fact, the only thing missing in a healthy mother's breast milk could be vitamin D. That's why many doctors suggest a vitamin D supplement for mothers who are breast-feeding.

Your child's brain is a biochemical machine. There's only one way your child can get those biochemicals—from the right nutrients in the right amounts.

Francine Prince and Harold Prince, Ph.D. in *Feed Your Kids Bright*

Breast-feeding for at least six months to a year is generally recommended. Then you can start adding solids such as instant rice, barley or corn cereal; cooked and pureed vegetables; pureed fruit; and then finely grated or mashed meats—important for their iron supply. Alternatively, of course, you can buy prepared baby food at the supermarket.

From the age of one onwards ensure that your toddler's diet includes:

▲ a balance of fish, beans, peas, lentils, soya and dairy products. An adequate supply of fish oil (the type found in sardines and salmon) and linoleic acid (as found in leafy green vegetables, fruits, dairy foods and vegetable oil) is important. Research now shows that children — with their 'nutrition hungry' brains — should NOT be put on a low fat diet.

▲ foods rich in zinc, such as chicken and fish. Even a mild deficiency in zinc can cause reduced memory ability.

▲ a breakfast cereal fortified with vitamins and minerals and milk followed by half a banana or a sliced apple or orange. The banana provides potassium—vital for brain function. The milk provides vitamins, minerals, calcium and protein. The cereal provides carbohydrates for energy.

▲ snacks of whole wheat bread and fresh fruit instead of sugar-laden foods such as chocolate cookies.

▲ complex carbohydrates such as bread, pasta and potatoes in their lunch.

Keep the chocolates, soft drinks and candies to a minimum—the excess sugar actually robs the body of key nutrients.

Adequate amounts of those nutrients vital to both brain and body . . . must be fed to the infant after birth, especially during the first three years of life. It will make all the difference, in the long run, to the child's mental capabilities.

Dr. Brian and Roberta Morgan in *Brain Food*

12. From eighteen months on

What do you have to look forward to?

> *Children can learn almost anything if they are dancing, tasting, touching, hearing, seeing and feeling information.*
>
> Jean Houston

Month after month you'll be observing milestone after milestone as your child continually acquires new skills. He'll be zooming through a period of tremendous curiosity in the next few years.

Developing the senses

Up until now, baby has been observing cause and effect: "I knock an egg off the table on to the floor and it breaks and splatters. I turn on the tap and water comes out." But generally at this age, he starts becoming a problem-solver: he starts a much higher level of thinking.

> *Most kids hear what you say; some kids do what you say; but all kids do what you do.*
>
> Kathleen Theisen

And he starts becoming very curious about everything. Let him satisfy his curiosity. Have him outdoors as much as possible. Within your budget provide him with a range of simple toys that will enable him to experiment with all his senses:

Kindergarten blocks in squares, oblongs, triangles, half-circles, diagonals, curves and pillars; inlaid puzzles with large pieces that can be removed; simple instruments, such as a small xylophone, bells, tambourine, triangle, drum; a form board with simple geometric shapes; a giant magnet; magnifying glass; flashlight, take-apart trucks and toys; and, if you can afford it or make it out of an old packing case, a playhouse.

> *The best inheritance a parent can give his or her child is a few minutes of time each day.*
>
> O. A. Batista

Spend a few minutes rolling around the floor with your 18-month-old. You'll be increasing her confidence to tackle many other 'academic' problems. Rolling around the floor helps to make your child more relaxed and physically confident. It helps her to overcome an instinctive 'fight or flight' reflex she was born with: the Moro reflex.

Emotional development

One key transition period comes when baby starts to pull himself up and to walk with support but before he can walk reasonably well by himself. At this in-between stage, falls are inevitable. So are genuine cries when he hurts himself. But by making those cries he soon perceives that crying may guarantee attention.

> *If we think we can we will. If we think we can't we won't. All that stands between ourselves and our capabilities are our perceptions of who we are and what we can do.*
>
> H. Stephen Glenn and Jane Nelson in *Raising Self-Reliant Children in a Self-Indulgent World*

Common sense tells us to try and distinguish between a genuine cry of pain and one that is only to gain attention. In theory at least, try and treat minimal cries with minimal response.

If it's a genuine distress call, obviously immediate comfort is called for. But if it's a minor matter, try to treat it as such without too much personal attention, except a verbal acknowledgment: "Oops, you've fallen down again. I bet you can stand up and try again." Treat minor bumps and falls in a matter-of-fact, "you'll be O. K. soon" way.

Recalling the day: Just after the bath and before bed, perhaps while you are putting on your toddler's pyjamas, pick out a few highlights of the day and remind him of them. It might be a visit, a shopping trip, an ice cream, a game —even breakfast. The ability to replay visual images will be a critical memory skill in the future. Building memory skills can be started early.

Mirror Games: Let your older toddler discover about himself through occasional use of both a full-length and hand mirror. He'll want to dance and pose and act out situations. This lets him see his whole body in action. The more he learns about himself, the more assurance he will have later in new situations.

Developing music and listening skills

Rhyming stories and cassettes are great for teaching reading, music and poetry. Start with nursery rhymes—as early as you like.

Add plenty of rhyme and rhythm into a child's life. Introduce rhyming stories and cassettes: *Three Blind Mice, Jack and Jill, Humpty Dumpty* and *The Three Little Pigs.*

Choose Dr. Seuss beginner books, which combine rhyme, wonderful rhythm and fantasy, both in words and pictures. The *Dr. Seuss Sleep Book, The Cat In The Hat* and *The Cat In The Hat Came Back* are excellent. And if you can play the piano, introduce your daughter to *Twinkle, Twinkle Little Star.*

Encouraging creative play

Your brain can keep learning from birth till the end of life.

Marian Diamond in *Enriching Heredity*

Here are some creative activities you can try with your 18-month-old.

Shopping at home: After a visit to the supermarket, you can make a similar 'trip' at home. Using a stroller or brick cart, you can travel from room to room (department to department), collecting a loaf of bread, a packet of soup, some orange juice, etc. A good game to play just before lunch—then you can eat the items you bought.

Colors: Colors are best taught one at a time, especially as the idea of 'blueness' is not so obvious to a baby. Start with a favorite toy and compare it directly with something else, e.g. "This car is red. So is this ball. They are both red." Then find as many examples of the color red over the next few days, including offering him red things: a mug, gloves, coat, etc.

Approaching the age of two

The greatest unexplored territory in the world is the space between our ears.

Bill O'Brien,
Chief Executive Officer,
Hanover Insurance

Baby's spoken vocabulary will probably increase to between 200 and 300 words by his second birthday. It may be higher. And he'll be absorbing hundreds more. He'll be able to point to several of his body parts, use his own name, follow some simple directions and speak some fairly complete sentences.

By the same landmark, he will generally be able to jump with both feet together, throw a ball underarm, scribble and draw lines with crayons, build a tower of five to six cubes, turn the pages of a book one at a time, use a spoon to eat, drink from a cup using one hand, and pull off his socks, shoes and pants.

> **If I had my child to raise over again**
>
> *If I had my child to raise all over again,*
> *I'd finger paint more and point the finger less,*
> *I'd do less correcting and more connecting.*
> *I'd take my eyes off my watch and watch with my eyes.*
> *I would care to know less, and know to care more.*
> *I'd take more hikes and fly more kites.*
> *I'd stop playing serious and seriously play.*
> *I'd run through more fields, and gaze at more stars.*
> *I'd do more hugging, and less tugging.*
> *I would be firm less often, and affirm much more.*
> *I'd build self-esteem first, and the house later.*
> *I'd teach less about the love of power,*
> *And more about the power of love.*
>
> Diane Loomans in *Full Esteem Ahead*

Remember the importance of positive encouragement. If your child says, "I goed to the store," don't tell her that's wrong. Instead try: "You went to the store didn't you? And I went too. Tomorrow we'll both go to the store again."

Turn language and learning into fun games, guessing games. "These are my eyes. And this is my nose. Have you got eyes? Where are they? Have you got a nose? Where is it?"

And then?

Step up to *FUNdamentals*

First FUNdamentals is just a beginning—first steps to get your child off to a flying start in life. You have moved along the learning curve from the very first days you brought your baby home, to the time when she's become a personality, when she's showing her individual characteristics and aptitudes.

YOUR next step is to progress to the complete *Accelerated Learning FUNdamentals* program—a child development system containing more than 1,000 games and activities.

The goal of *FUNdamentals* is balance—to help your child become a truly 'rounded' individual. A child who will not only be able to read, and write and do basic mathematics before starting school, but will also be acquiring:

- **self-esteem**
- **concentration**
- **creativity**
- **clear thinking**
- **basic values**
- **persistence**
- **musical sense**
- **responsibility**
- **money sense**
- **self-confidence.**

FUNdamentals achieves the above through the use of:

ACTIVITY CARDS—hundreds of quick reference cards providing hours of pleasure for the home and car.

VIDEO—containing invaluable common sense advice from international child development experts.

ILLUSTRATED GUIDEBOOK—which steers you through all the stages of development.

WORD CARDS—over 600 to help teach early reading through both phonics and whole words.

BOARD GAMES—reading, writing and math made fun!

With *FUNdamentals* you'll never wonder "What can we do now?" You'll have thousands of ideas and games at your fingertips—years of enjoyable activities that will systematically develop the skills, characteristics and values that lead to a successful, happy, well-rounded child. **YOUR child.**

> *The illiterate of the 21st Century will not be the individual who cannot read and write but the one who cannot learn, unlearn and relearn.*
>
> Alvin Toffler

Marking the real first birthday

What to do

Children love birthday parties, but how many of them get to celebrate their own birth day? Compile a scrapbook or album of that very first day or week: perhaps starting with photographs showing Mom pregnant, and then the first shots of baby himself. And how about adding in all the greeting cards and telegrams? Letters from friends? Copies of the newspaper birth notice?

How it helps your child to learn

Self-esteem begins with a child's appreciation of himself or herself—from the very start.

Self-esteem

Special tip

Make a point of getting photos taken of you sitting up in bed with baby from the very first week.

And another thing!

Keep records of each birthday, bring them out each year as you talk about progress from one year to the next.

First steps to language

What to do

From the start of life, get into the habit of talking to your baby *about what is happening right here and now.* Just because the baby cannot talk, it does not mean that he cannot listen. But even as late as two years of age, babies cannot understand references to objects that are not present or events that are even half a day into the future.

How it helps your child to learn

Listening to good speech is the first step towards linguistic intelligence. If a child hears good speech she can imitate it.

How to proceed

Talk specifically about what you are doing as you are doing it:

"Now Mommy's changing your diapers (or nappy)."

"Now Karen is going to eat."

Give reason for things you are doing. It's the first lesson in cause and effect.

"This is your bath. And this is nice warm water in it. I'll feel it first to make sure it's not too hot."

Speech

Special tip

If you or your friends speak a foreign language, encourage its use in talking to baby. Linguistic patterns start early.

And another thing!

Don't over-stimulate baby in the first few months by talking too loudly. Communicate quietly.

First steps to music

What to do

Select suitable music on cassette or compact disc and play it unobtrusively in the background.

Play good music perhaps two or three times a day: in the morning, at lunchtimes and at night when he's going to bed. About 20 minutes' music at a time, but more won't hurt.

How it helps your child to learn

He'll develop an early love of good music and also develop 'perfect pitch.' Sing, hum or dance along with the music so he knows it spells enjoyment and fun.

How to start

Examples of soothing background music, such as:

Peer Gynt Suite by Grieg.

The Swan from *The Carnival of The Animals* by Saint-Saens.

The second movement from the *Clarinet Quintet* by Mozart.

The Four Seasons by Vivaldi.

Watermark by Enja.

No Blue Thing by Ray Lynch.

Pastoral Symphony by Beethoven.

Listening, musical skills

Special tip

Don't feel you have to play only classical music, but don't choose anything too loud. Pleasant melodies rather than hard rock!

And another thing!

Include music from your own cultural background—Salsa, Spanish, Calypso or folk, for instance.

Choosing the first toys

What to do

Early toys should have strong visual appeal, with sharp black-and-white contrasts or bright colors like reds, blues, greens, yellows and oranges. Between three and six months, toys should have interesting textures as baby starts exploring with her hands. From six to nine months, choose toys with moving pieces to explore. By the end of the year: pick toys that nest, stack and move in interesting ways when handled.

How it helps your child to learn

Age-appropriate toys help baby move on to the next level of development.

All senses

Special tip

Buy toys that have multiple uses. Make them small enough to be grasped, so they can be played with—in the crib or on the floor.

And another thing!

In the first year, make sure all toys are too large to swallow, have no sharp edges and are practically unbreakable.

The right environment

What to do

From the outset, provide baby with a stimulating environment. You can make her room more colorful with plants and posters, colored bottles on the window sill and interesting shapes on the wallpaper. Wind chimes make pleasant sounds. And placing a bird-feeder outside her window can encourage an interest in the natural world.

How it helps your child to learn

The more varied and pleasant the stimulation, the better the growth of basic brain pathways.

Senses- sight & hearing

Special tip

Animal scenes, bright paintings and posters are ideal.

And another thing!

While children like sharp visual contrasts, they prefer to settle into sleep with dimmed light. So consider fitting a dimmer switch.

Move the crib regularly

What to do

For the first nine months of his life, move baby's crib to a new position once a week. Sometimes position it so he can see out of the window; other times, face the door, the mirror or some of the paintings or decorations around the room.

How it helps your child to learn

A regular change of location will enable him to change both his view and his perspective. It's thus another way to develop both visual and spatial perception. Imagine how bored you would be if your view was the same every day.

Senses – sight, spatial intelligence

Special tip

After eight or nine months most babies prefer their routine to be more established, with their cribs in one position.

And another thing!

If you have several paintings or prints change their position every few weeks so that each one has a turn in the nursery.

Stimulating the senses

What to do

From the very first days with your baby, try to captivate his interest with a series of simple activities to stimulate each of his senses: one visual, one auditory, one smell, one movement, one taste and one touch game per session. Take only about a minute with each, so the whole session lasts no longer than six minutes. Repeat three times a day: before the main feeding times.

How it helps your child to learn

A child learns through all five senses, and movement. The more each sense is stimulated the more it opens up the pathways to each part of the brain. But be sensitive to baby's reactions—continue only if he's relaxed.

Sample games

Visual game: Show baby a 'visual stimulator': a bull's-eye or checkerboard pattern.

Touch: A minute of skin stroking, starting from the back of the head and moving down the body. Blow on her toes or tummy.

Hearing: Use a rattle or bells.

Smelling: Expose her to some pleasant spices, perfumes and herbs.

Taste: Dip a cotton bud in orange juice, or another safe taste. Place on tongue.

Movement: Rocking.

All senses

Special tip

Except for gentle body massage, which can be longer, one minute is long enough for any segment. But vary the order.

And another thing!

Always tell baby what she is experiencing: "This is cinnamon. This is orange juice. This is the sound of a tiny bell."

Recording each milestone

What to do

Even if you haven't made a special birthday album, take photos of every milestone in development: soon after birth, the first time she lifts her head and chest off the ground while lying on her stomach; the first time she handles objects; sits alone; takes her first steps; walks freely; runs; pulls a cart or rides a tricycle.

How it helps your child to learn

This is a tremendous aid to self-esteem. As your infant matures she can see and appreciate her own unique development as a person.

Self-esteem, confidence

Special tip

Keep a record of times and dates of each milestone and write them in your album or scrapbook.

And another thing!

As she gets older involve her in choosing and sticking in the photos. Regularly look at the book talking about what happened and who was there.

Early exercises

What to do

Even though she can't walk for several months, baby still enjoys exercise from the start. You can help her 'cycle' by exercising her legs while she's lying on her back; exercise her arms the same way. Combine leg and arm stretches; lift her legs a few inches off the floor or pull her gently to a standing position by holding both her arms firmly and then letting her practise deep-knee bends.

How it helps your child to learn

Early 'motor' actions lay down the 'muscle memory' through which much other learning takes place.

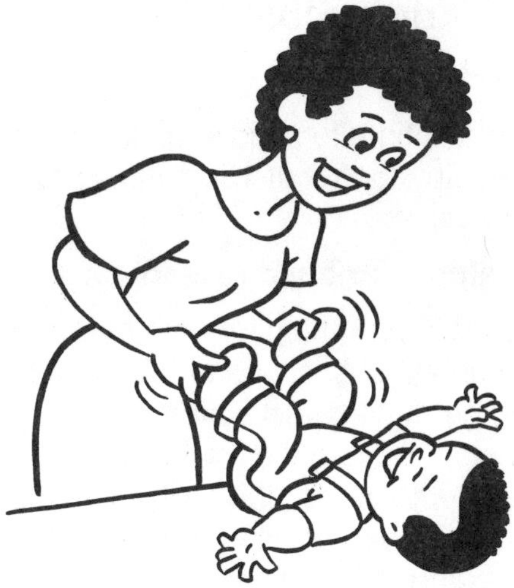

Physical skills

Special tip

Crawling starts earlier if she has something to crawl towards like a rattle shaken just out of reach or outstretched arms.

And another thing!

After five months you can add in aeroplane spins and roll her on her tummy over a big ball or over one of her tactile toys.

Getting into the swim

What to do

Babies can learn to swim almost from the moment of birth. If you have a warm spa pool nearby, consider introducing your baby to it as early as you like—and get in it with him. Alternatively, seek out a suitable 'Baby and Me' swimming class. If you like the idea of early swimming, do it before your baby completes his first two months. During that time he has a built-in reflex that enables him to 'dog paddle' in water.

How it helps your child to learn

Swimming involves almost every muscle. Babies who swim also tend to walk early and coordinate well.

Physical skills

Special tip

Before enrolling your baby in a swim class, check the instructor's methods. Not all instructors are great with infants.

And another thing!

Being in a pool with baby is great for early parent-child bonding. Make sure to spend a lot of that time face to face and smiling.

Rockin' and rubbin'

What to do

Try and make time to cuddle, rock, stroke and massage your new baby for about 15 minutes at a time and four times a day.

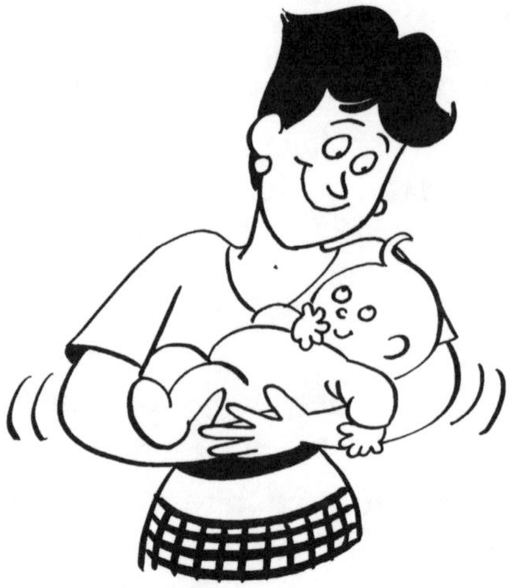

How it helps your child to learn

This is not only soothing for both parent and child, but we now know that this type of regular activity helps greatly in promoting a vital type of brain growth: the part that helps a child coordinate movements and to learn. Controlled tests at the University of Texas have shown that premature babies, in particular, benefit from rocking, rolling, rubbing and stroking.

Brain capacity

Special tip

Rocking, in particular, stimulates the nervous system linking the ear and the part of the brain that deals with balance.

And another thing!

Later, from around four months, hold baby securely and give her regular 'aeroplane spins'—also good for stimulating balance.

As simple as black and white

What to do

An optional, highly recommended companion to this program is a set of eight double-sided cards with bold black & white illustrations on each side. Attach card numbers 1-8 to baby's crib so she can see them from birth. After about six weeks switch to cards No. 9-16.

How it helps your child to learn

This will pay off later with much better visual ability. Baby's visual pathways have six levels, each one handling a different type of vision. Thus one level processes dots, another squares, another horizontal stripes and yet another vertical stripes.

Senses – sight

Special tip

Amazingly, if a baby saw only horizontal stripes for the first two years, she would not have the ability to see vertical stripes.

And another thing!

Because of the importance of contrasts, a black-and-white panda or panda puppet should be one of your child's first toys.

First steps to walking

What to do

Infants as young as two weeks can be encouraged to walk. Simply hold your baby under his arms and encourage him to imitate walking movements on a firm, flat surface—preferably with bare feet and in a warm room. The movement is called reflex stepping, and it is particularly strong between two and eight weeks of age.

How it helps your child to learn

Some youngsters who do reflex stepping between two and eight weeks begin walking at a much earlier age. Five out of six in one test were walking at 10 months.

Physical skills

Special tip

Even as early as two weeks, most babies like to be held under the arms and bounced on their parents' laps.

And another thing!

Bouncing on your lap won't make your baby bow-legged. In fact, the exercise helps his legs get stronger.

Barefoot exploration

What to do

As long as the baby is inside and the temperature is comfortable, consider leaving her mostly barefoot for the first two years of life. And even outside, if the temperature is not cold and the underfoot area is safe (grass or sand), let her explore her environment in bare feet.

How it helps your child to learn

A young child absorbs experiences through all her senses and that includes the sense of touch. This sense is very well developed early in life, even before the visual and auditory pathways are fully developed.

Senses – touch

Special tip

Don't put booties, socks or mittens on baby when you're playing with her feet or hands. It cuts down the feel and the fun!

And another thing!

Even good sneakers and shoes — those with gripping soles — make physical movement more difficult for a child. Barefoot is best.

Making your first mobile

What to do

Attach a mobile with brightly contrasting colors to the crib. Use bold drawings that are similar to the top half of the human face (see card 11). At three weeks baby will only look at the mobile and not touch it, so there is no need to worry about sturdiness. String the contrasting items about 10 inches from baby's eyes (30 cm). Place most items on the right or the left, not directly overhead.

How it helps your child to learn

After sucking, your baby's first exploration starts with visual examination of the near environment.

Senses – sight

Special tip

Leave a good quality, unbreakable mirror fastened to the inside of the crib. Its reflections provide even more to look at.

And another thing!

Bold-picture alphabet friezes are good on non-checker-boarded walls. And tell baby the words the pictures depict: apple, ball, etc.

Add texture to pictures

What to do

Try to ensure that some of your early 'visual stimulation' introduces textures as well. Put up some pictures that show different textures. You can do this by drawing or cutting out big, clear pictures of animals, flowers or clown faces and adding your own 'extras': cotton wool for a bunny's tail, a red-colored table tennis ball for a clown's nose, some real dried leaves with trees.

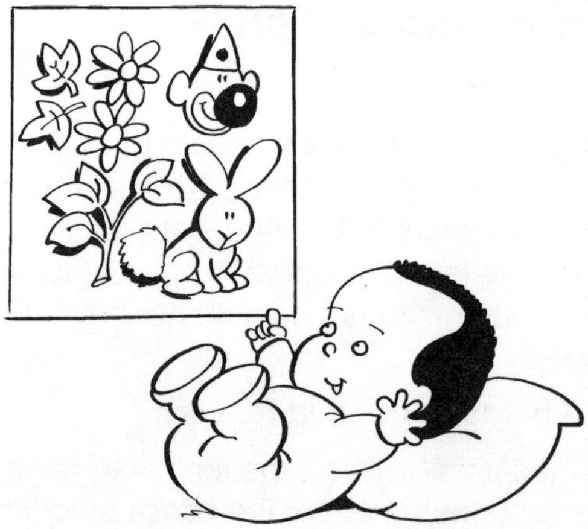

How it helps your child to learn

This adds three dimensions to your baby's early visual fields and it helps develop good spatial awareness.

Senses – sight, spatial intelligence

Special tip

Talk to your baby about what she can see: the fluffy bunny's tail, the smiling clown's face, the leaves on the tree.

And another thing!

Keep 3D posters out of baby's reach so she can't grasp your small additions and possibly choke on them.

First conversation

What to do

When your baby is lying or sitting facing you, make direct eye contact. Then begin to make a simple face—pulling your tongue in and out, for example, or opening and shutting your mouth. Watch to see if your baby copies you. Even very young babies can respond to faces and voices in subtle ways. So watch carefully for them.

How it helps your child to learn

Your baby learns to pay attention to your face for clues. He also learns that his response pleases you. It's the start of two way communication. **If your baby feels good *while* he's learning, he will feel good *about* learning.**

Concentration, social skills

Special tip

Babies will also 'respond' non-verbally to your conversation. So pause after you say something, and wait for signs of his 'reply.'

And another thing!

When he does respond, vary the faces—raise your eyebrows, smile, make whispering sounds and repeat any actions that make him interested.

Step up the visual contrast

What to do

If baby has been exposed to regular visual stimulation from birth, he is ready for much more spectacular progress. Between one and three months. His field of vision will expand from about 15 in. (37 cm) to around 10 feet (3 meters). From six weeks, use black-and-white crib cards with finer shapes.

Reduced pattern.

How it helps your child to learn

The smaller patterns help him to increase his visual discrimination. Encourage eye-tracking by deliberately moving your head slowly from side to side across his field of vision.

Senses – sight, spatial intelligence

Special tip

Keep bright toys, with contrasting colors, within baby's reach as he passes six weeks and is beginning to see better.

And another thing!

Your baby can now see the ceiling, so consider sticking brightly colored shapes on the ceiling above the crib, or on the wall.

Make your own tactile toy

What to do

Take a large sweatsock or a man's long walking sock. On the outside sew an array of textures—horizontal stripes of different colors in corduroy, silk, toweling, velvet, satin, plaid and denim. Turn the foot of the sock into a face by sewing on black-and-white eyes, a red mouth and some colored wool for hair. Stuff with old tights, for instance, perhaps include a small bell inside.

How it helps your child to learn

This enables a baby to develop his tactile ability, his sense of touch and feel.

Senses – touch

Special tip

Use your ingenuity to turn a similar toy into a colorful, friendly snake or caterpillar, with its own name.

And another thing!

When you first introduce a tactile toy, take baby's hands and get him to feel each piece of fabric as you tell him what it is.

Bringing the hands into play

What to do

From the time he is two months old, baby becomes fascinated with his own hands. You can help his eye-hand coordination with several simple steps. Invest in the kind of wrist rattles which attach to the wrist by Velcro (many commercial models come with animal faces, and a black-and-white panda is especially appealing). Move his hands over his own body, naming each part. Regularly put your fingers in his grasp.

How it helps your child to learn

This is great for eye-hand coordination, which in turn is essential later for reading, writing, crawling and walking.

Physical skills

Special tip

Baby's fists don't start to relax until at least one month. Even though he won't be able to hold them place rattles and smaller toys in his hand.

And another thing!

Make sure that none of his playthings have buttons or bells that can come off and be swallowed.

From mobile to crib gym

What to do

As soon as baby starts reaching for her mobile, often as early as eight to 10 weeks, buy or construct a much more permanent 'crib gym.' You'll find baby not only looking at nearby bright objects, but striking, 'batting' or swiping at them with her hands. She is no longer content to look, she wants to explore. And she can do this best if she can easily grasp safe objects.

How it helps your child to learn

A vital stage in encouraging eye-hand coordination. Reaching for objects helps converge her eyes.

How to make one

Baby needs something which will stand up to being batted and later grasped. So make sure the objects are securely attached to a pole or strong nylon cable strung across the cot. Brightly colored objects, balls or rattle rings can be threaded onto strong string securely.

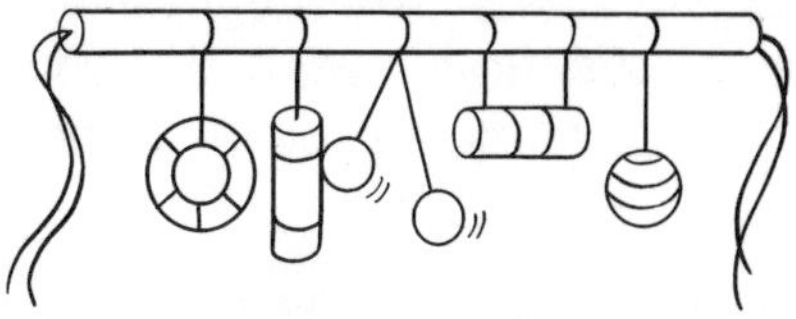

NOTE: Any form of cord can be **extremely** dangerous if it comes loose. Secure fitting is vital.

Senses – sight, physical skills

Special tip

A rattle or wooden spoon can be introduced to baby by eight weeks but she will not be able to hold it until around 14 weeks.

And another thing!

You can also help visual stimulation by drawing a bright puppet face on a paper plate and moving it around near baby's face.

The tickling monster

What to do

Put your baby on his back. Kneel beside him, smile as you look into his eyes, and say "Let's play *Here's the tickling monster.* Here he comes." Bring your hand into view, close to your face, wriggling your fingers. As you lower your hand to tickle the baby, make a pleasant whistling or cooing sound, lowering the pitch as you move towards the baby.

How it helps your child to learn

Apart from the fun involved, it helps introduce the spirit of cooperation in play and the anticipation builds memory skills. So be consistent in the way you play the game.

Physical skills

Special tip

Consistent routines help baby begin to make sense of the world. So, try to establish routines for breakfast, bathtime, bedtime etc.

And another thing!

Some babies are more ticklish than others. Some like to be naked, others clothed. So be sensitive and adapt to his preferences.

Another vital sense

What to do

Stimulate your baby's sense of smell by spraying cotton balls with mother's perfume and father's aftershave lotion. Add to the stimulation by using sweet-smelling fruits and flowers and a variety of kitchen smells, such as cinnamon, nutmeg and honey. Use different ones each day, so you can mention them by name as you waft each smell under his nose two or three times.

How it helps your child to learn

Helps develop baby's olfactory sense, which is otherwise often the least developed of the senses.

Senses – smell

Special tip

Include your own 'personal smells' — perfume, deodorant, powder and lipstick — in each game until he is used to them.

And another thing!

If leaving baby with a sitter, leave some fabric with your own perfume in baby's bedroom, as a reminder of your presence.

Bouncing baby to music

What to do

Put on a music tape or compact disc or get yourself into a singing mood. Bounce baby on your knee or cross your legs and hold his arms as you sit him on your foot. Bounce him in time to the music or song. Pay attention to his signals. Let him see he can influence what happens. For example, if he continues to bounce when you stop, comment, "So you want to bounce some more?" and continue.

How it helps your child to learn

Develops a sense of rhythm and links it to bodily movement—the forerunner to dancing.

Musical, physical skills

Special tip

Try baby bouncing on your knee so he can see himself in the mirror.

And another thing!

As a variation, with music playing, simply hold baby as you would a ballroom dancing partner and dance around the room.

Start the reading early

What to do

It's almost never too early to start reading to your child. When she's sitting on your knee, feeding or propped up on cushions, read to her from a variety of books. Start with books that feature only simple, bold pictures, then pictures with 'label' words, then moving on to simple stories. Even though she can't speak, she is absorbing knowledge from the outset.

THAT'S A JUICY RED APPLE, AND THAT'S A BIG BLUE BALL

How it helps your child to learn

A child who is read to appreciates from the start that books are sources of enjoyment and information. Your own joy in reading communicates these two concepts.

Speech, reading

Special tip

It's fine to use books that illustrate the alphabet with bold pictures. But concentrate on the words not the letters.

And another thing!

Point to the words and pictures in nursery rhymes, and then repeat the nursery rhymes when you are bathing your baby or playing.

A new use for books

What to do

Most of us think of books for reading. But invest in some good, thick card books from about four months and you'll find extra fascination. Babies are intrigued by movement and one of the first movements they can personally orchestrate (apart from 'batting' a mobile) is to turn over the pages of books (later they'll graduate to kitchen doors!). Choose books that have simple, colorful illustrations.

BOY! THIS SURE BEATS MILK AND VOMIT.

How it helps your child to learn

Turning books helps 'motor' development. The books are also good for 'gumming' before teething.

Physical skills & reading

Special tip

Make sure to use books that won't easily fall apart and are safe in the mouth, because they'll spend a good deal of time there.

And another thing!

Wipe the books regularly with a clean sponge, then dry with a clean cloth. You can't stop germs, but you can restrict their spread.

Names, names, names

What to do

Baby's understanding starts to blossom between eight and 12 months. He can't talk much but he begins to associate names with objects. So talk to him as often as you can about what he can see and touch. Tell him, in particular, about the parts of his body—especially his face. And as he starts to understand, prop him in front of a mirror and ask him to show you where his mouth is and his other body parts.

THESE ARE YOUR EYES AND THEY'RE BLUE!

How it helps your child to learn

Nouns are usually the first words to be learnt. And the easiest place to start is with the child's own body—bathtime is ideal for naming and counting.

Speech

Special tip

As soon as your child starts to understand the names of each body part, turn the teaching into questions: "Where are your eyes, your ears?"

And another thing!

Use meal time to label things, eg: "This is Mommy's spoon. Where's Helen's spoon? Here's Helen's plate." Label and talk **all** the time.

Make your own fun smock

What to do

Make your own black-and-white striped apron or a coloful smock with deep pockets. This will enable you to store an array of simple toys and effects: cassette tapes, bells, rattles, 'smelling and tasting bottles,' letters, numbers, word cards and anything else you need for stimulating baby.

AND NOW FOR ANOTHER MAGIC SMELL

How it helps your child to learn

By doing this, you're always ready to introduce some variety and, where needed, distraction. Often the simple act of being prepared makes it easier to ring the changes.

All senses

Special tip

Consider making several different colored shapes — triangles, diamonds, fruits — with Velcro backing. Stick them on your smock.

And another thing!

Some prefer a magic bag or box to a smock. Always include a mirror in your 'magic' bag so baby can watch himself.

The 'Give it to me' game

What to do

With your baby on the floor on his tummy, side or sitting, place a toy just out of her reach. Move the toy about and say something like: "Look at this. Would you like to have a look?" A dancing soft toy that you make 'talk' is particularly good for this. If your baby makes a sound or movement in response, give her the toy, saying "Here you are. You can have ..."

How it helps your child to learn

This simple routine helps your baby learn logically to attract attention by vocalizing and to communicate through sound and action.

Senses – sight, speech

Special tip

At the start, make it easier by holding a small toy just in front of your seated baby. If she moves towards it, give it to her.

And another thing!

You can make the game more 'educational' by repeating the toy's name clearly and precisely as you hand it to her.

Copy cat

What to do

Sit opposite your baby in his high chair. Give him a spoon and take a similar spoon yourself. Tap the spoon on the tray a couple of times. If he doesn't follow gently take his hand and guide it so he follows your actions.

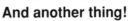

How it helps your child to learn

He's learning to pay attention, copy actions, take turns and communicate non-verbally.

Physical & social skills

Special tip

When he's comfortable with copying your actions, see if he can copy a specific number of taps. That's much more difficult.

And another thing!

The game can extend to copying clapping, waving, patting knees, stamping feet, touching ears, etc.

Start counting with the body

What to do

You can start teaching your infant basic mathematics by counting everything that is familiar to her. Again, start with her own body, "This is your nose. And this is your ear. You've got one nose, but you've got two ears. And these are your toes. You've got five toes on this foot and five toes on this one."

AND FIVE TOES ON THIS FOOT TOO

How it helps your child to learn

Mathematical concepts are learned easily if they are associated with specific objects, especially if those are as personal as eyes, ears, fingers and toes.

Math

Special tip

Action words, too, can be turned into counting games. "Let's walk up the stairs: one stair, two stairs, three stairs, four ..."

And another thing!

Count everything with your child: beans, buttons, spoons, knives, glasses, steps, stairs, stones, books and potatoes for dinner.

Up and down 'the hill'

What to do

When your infant is just starting to crawl, you can make the challenge ever more interesting by turning four cushions from a sofa into a three-tiered hill. First he can crawl up each level. You can then reverse the game by cutting up a large cardboard box (check that there are no staples sticking out), and turning it into a slide on to the cushions.

How it helps your child to learn

Crawling promotes one of the really important steps in brain development. The alternative use of left and right legs and arms integrates both sides of the brain.

Physical skills

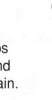

Special tip

When almost ready to crawl, often pushing baby's feet is all the help she needs—especially if inclined downhill.

And another thing!

An old table-top or plain door, lying on the floor but propped up at one end, is also a good aid to 'crawling down the slope.'

First ball games

What to do

Ball games can start at this stage, using big balls at first: ones that your baby can grasp with two hands. Sit him on the floor with legs apart and gently roll the ball between his legs, encouraging him to roll it back to you. It may take a few tries for him to get the idea, but persevere—and make it fun.

How it helps your child to learn

Each child needs to develop big muscle or 'big motor' abilities before he can handle more intricate maneuvers. He learns to roll a ball with his hands before he can grasp small knobs with his fingers.

Physical skills & spatial intelligence

Special tip

For another game, roll a ball just slightly out of your child's reach so that he has to crawl or walk after it to retrieve it.

And another thing!

Games with soft balls can be played inside but, if the weather permits, most of the games should also be played outdoors on the grass.

Puppet play

What to do

Make simple hand puppets from old socks or mittens. Stich on black eyes and nose and embroider a mouth in wool, perhaps adding woolly hair. Let your baby see what puppets can do: make them dance, sing, sleep and so on. The puppets should 'talk' to your baby as they play: "Hello, David, I'm Woof the dog. Do you want to see me dance? Look. I'm dancing. Will you help me sing?"

How it helps your child to learn

Great for creativity, developing imagination and for learning to pretend. Leave time for your child to respond to the puppet.

Creativity & musical skills

Special tip

Make-believe puppets encourage children to 'be' someone else and can help them understand how others think and feel.

And another thing!

Make musical puppets by sewing bells on them. Encourage his puppet to imitate yours, eg: "My puppet can scratch his head, can yours?"

The first steps

What to do

Most children take their first steps between nine and 14 months. When your child begins to show an interest in walking without holding on, encourage her. While she is standing and holding on to a chair or table kneel up to three feet (a meter) away from her, with your arms out towards her. When she reaches you, give her a big hug and plenty of congratulations. Gradually extend the distance.

How it helps your child

Walking is a mighty step forward—the opening of the road to full exploration of the environment.

Physical skills, spatial intelligence

Special tip

If someone else is present, make the reverse journey easy by turning the child around, towards the other person's outstretched arms.

And another thing!

Don't worry about the odd fall on to the carpet, but generally try to set up each milestone, so that she can succeed.

Up and away

What to do

Soon after a baby begins to crawl, he starts to discover his ability to climb. Assist it. Place a secure gate at the top of any stairs, and perhaps one three or four steps up, a large cushion at the bottom and let him go to it!

How it helps your child to learn

Climbing is great for exploring and for satisfying curiosity. While babies can learn to climb *up* stairs, they need a lot more practice before they can get *down*. Climbing also helps hand-eye-body coordination and confidence-building.

Physical skills, spatial intelligence

Special tip

Early on, help your infant get down stairs on his stomach feet first.

And another thing!

For stair climbing teach your infant how to bend and flex his legs by holding him and demonstrating on the stairs.

The Peepo or Peeko game

What to do

Sit your baby on the floor. Play, talk and smile at him to get his attention. Cover your head with a scarf but continue to talk to him: "Can Peter find me? Where's Daddy gone?" Wait a few seconds, then quickly remove the scarf, saying "Peepo" or "Peeko." You can play 'Peepo' by moving behind a chair or out into the hall, behind curtains or hiding behind another person.

How it helps your child to learn

This helps in many ways: to relate and communicate with others through play; to anticipate, imitate and co-operate; to recognize and respond to his own name. It also adds to his sense of curiosity.

Curiosity, thinking

Special tip

For a baby who appears alarmed by his parent's face disappearing, just cover your eyes with your hands.

And another thing!

You can also play by crawling away from your baby but stopping to look back and saying "Peepo—come and get me."

Hide and seek with toys

What to do

Choose a few toys that you know will capture your child's interest. A small toy that squeaks can be very good for this game. Let your child watch as you hide a toy under a cloth, cushion or cup. You'll have to get his attention by squeaking the toy and saying something like, "Look, James, where did it go?" When he uncovers the toy, it's important to respond enthusiastically, "There, you found it!"

How it helps your child to learn

He learns that hiding objects does not make them disappear. It also helps him to pay attention.

Memory & concentration

Special tip

A good object to hide is a musical toy that can be wound up and will keep playing after it has been hidden.

And another thing!

Let him see himself in a mirror. Cover it up, then take the cloth away saying "Look, there's Simon." Next time, let him work out how to see himself.

Stacking toys

What to do

As she gains more control of grasping, introduce stacking toys, such as large plastic cups or cones that can fit inside each other. See if she can put them together and pull them apart. If it's too difficult at first, give her only two at a time.

How it helps your child to learn

Hand-eye coordination is so important for many activities: walking, running, drawing, writing. This is also an early lesson in cause-and-effect logic.

Physical skills & logic

Special tip

Stack them in a tower and let baby knock them down —show her how if you have to.

And another thing!

Preferably each stacking plaything should be small enough for baby to hold in one hand, but not so small that she can swallow it.

Building words on the actions

What to do

The 12 to 18 month walking period is a great time to build new words on the actions your child is doing. When he walks around the room, tell him what he has done, "Great. You just walked around the room." If you're going outside, tell him, "Let's go outside now. But it's a little cold. So let's put on your mittens."

IT'S COLD OUTSIDE LET'S WEAR OUR MITTENS

How it helps your child to learn

Your child will build word patterns much more easily if they relate to what he is doing and if he learns them while he is doing a particular action. *Experience, then label* is a key principle in learning.

Speech

Special tip

Build on what he can see, too. "That's a big dog. It's a brown and white dog. We call it a collie dog."

And another thing!

Don't worry that your child can't yet repeat everything he is told. Rest assured, he'll understand much more than he can speak.

Linking words with toys

What to do

From about 12 months, collect some playthings together, start with three and tell your baby the name of each. Let her handle and play with them for a while. Then say, "Where's the car?" Give her time to look at the car, touch it or maybe pick it up. If not, then you pick it up and say, "Here's the car," as you give it to her. Let her handle it as you name it again.

How it helps your child to learn

This helps your child to combine looking and listening—skills which are essential for reading and learning. It also helps associate key words with objects.

Speech, listening

Special tip

Play the game with people, too. If others are in the room simply ask, "Where's Daddy?" Or "Where's ...?"

And another thing!

You are not expecting the child to talk at this stage. But remember, she will understand many words well before she can speak them.

The first peg board

What to do

Some time between 12 and 18 months, your child will learn to put up to six large round pegs into a peg board. So provide him with a plastic or bright wooden peg board for his first birthday. Show him how to grasp the pegs first, then knock them together and gradually put each of them into a hole.

How it helps your child to learn

Learning to put large round pegs into the holes in a peg board is an important milestone. It means that baby's eye-hand coordination is coming together fine—well on the way to later writing ability.

Physical & writing skills

Special tip

Don't try to force the pace. Most children can do this by 18 months; some sooner, some later. Simply provide the opportunity.

And another thing!

Most children move on to peg boards after learning to stack two or more things together and mastering a two-handed drinking cup.

Learning affection

What to do

As your baby plays with soft toys, talk to her about what she is doing. "Bear feels soft/warm/furry… he feels good." Vary the tone of your voice with each toy. Talk in a soft and gentle whisper for a soft, fluffy toy such as a teddy bear, or in a bright voice for a colorful fabric toy such as a clown. After a while, suggest your baby might like to cuddle or stroke a toy or talk to it.

How it helps your child to learn

It's important for your child to understand the name for each feeling, and that feelings are OK. Say, for example, "Catherine is angry that Susan took her toy. Let's ask for it back nicely."

Speech

Special tip

Play-act with toys. Make one fall over, and say, "Teddy's hurt himself. Let's make him better." "Teddy's dancing. He's happy."

And another thing!

Take every opportunity to comment on your child's feelings. Use dolls and toys to get him to understand other peoples' feelings.

Busy boxes

What to do

From his first birthday, you'll find plenty of child development learning toys which incorporate several interactive items: flexible punch-balls for hitting, plastic telephone dials, switches that turn up and down, disks that spin round and other segments that slide. They're an excellent investment. Show him how each action works—and then let him get on with it.

How it helps your child to learn

All these activities will be needed as he grows: turning on lights, dialling a telephone and sliding doors. These toys provide an excellent safe way to start.

Physical skills

Special tip

Big plastic zip fasteners are good for small-muscle manipulation, but smaller metal zips can pinch small fingers.

And another thing!

If your child needs help, show him how to hit, slide, push and turn—the normal advancing degree of difficulty.

Stringing big beads

What to do

Some time between 15 and 18 months, most infants learn to string large beads together. But at this age you must start with very large 'beads,' either plastic or wooden with holes over half an inch (1cm.) wide and a good thick shoe lace. Tie a big knot in one end of the lace and show your child how to thread each separate item.

How it helps your child to learn

Just as round peg-boards encourage large motor skills, threading beads develops similar coordination —another step towards painting and writing.

Physical and writing skills

Special tip

By the same age, children should learn to wash and dry hands, peel a banana (if you start it) and unwrap simple packages.

And another thing!

Between one and two give plenty of opportunity for pushing and pulling practice with toys: cars, carts, anything with wheels.

Pointing together

What to do

Choose a book with simple, clear pictures of everyday objects. It's best if there is only one object on a page. Sit with your baby on your knee, open the book and wait for your baby to touch a picture. You then point to the picture he's interested in and talk to him about it, stressing the object's name and interesting points about it. "That's an apple. It's a big red apple. Apples are good to eat. Yummy."

How it helps your child to learn

It helps him to pay attention, to focus on interesting points. And it all helps speech growth.

Speech, reading

Special tip

It helps if you look and talk about pictures together when it's quiet and there are no noisy distractions.

And another thing!

After this type of reading exercise, search out real-life objects that he's been looking at, so he sees that books are guides to reality.

The first puzzles

What to do

Between12 months and two years, it's time to introduce some simple puzzles: bright shapes, cut out of wood so that they can fit easily into the same shaped hole. At first try puzzles containing only two or three large pieces: perhaps circles, squares and triangles. Pieces with large knobs are best.

How it helps your child to learn

Putting puzzles together teaches elementary logic. And by feeling the knob to put pieces in position the infant develops skills that will later help hold a pencil.

Thinking, writing

Special tip

Don't move on to multiple-piece puzzles until your child is very confident in assembling two and three-piece sets.

And another thing!

Between one and two, introduce blocks, stacking blocks, linking blocks and plastic pieces that snap together and pull apart.

Picture alphabet books

What to do

Alphabet books, with a single color illustration to each page, can be introduced from one year. When reading them at first make them very simple, saying only what appears, such as "A is for apple. B is for ball." Don't be afraid to mix up the 'proper' name for the letter with the different sounds, so that you can say either: "C (see) is for carrot," or "Kih is for carrot."

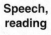

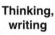

How it helps your child to learn

The 26 letters in the alphabet make up all 44 basic sounds in the language. Learning the alphabet along with basic words is one of the keys to linguistic ability.

Speech, reading

Special tip

If you haven't already done so, pin an alphabet poster or frieze on the nursery wall and use it to reinforce sounds and pictures.

And another thing!

From about 18 months of age, start singing the alphabet song to her: "A, B, C, D, E, F, G . . . H, I, J, K, L, M, N, O, P . . ."

Problem!

What to do

He can see it but he can't get it. Put some sultanas or little cheese biscuits into a clear plastic bottle. Ask him "How will you get them out?" If he gets frustrated, put the jar on its side to make it easier.

How it helps your child to learn

It's an introduction to problem solving. So is hiding toys under a drying cloth,wrapping toys in old Christmas paper, or dropping small objects through a hole in the lid of a box or any form of hunt the object. Children who see solving problems as fun are developing a positive attitude for the future.

Concentration

Special tip

Put a lid on the bottle and give one obvious turn to make the game harder.

And another thing!

A variation is to hide a grape under one of two cups. Then ask where it's gone. Think of some more puzzles like this.

Experiments

What to do

Look for **every** opportunity to encourage experimentation. Some ideas:

- Filling a series of different size containers with sand or earth with different tools—a spoon, stick, ruler, fork.
- Sorting apples and oranges. Sorting out socks in the laundry.
- Collecting a series of objects with holes in them and seeing which will fit over an arm, a finger, a stick.
- Building up plastic food boxes, or cardboard cartons.

How it helps your child to learn

Curiosity and trial and error is the basis for learning.

Creativity, math

Special tip

Talk about the textures she's feeling, and emphasize directional words, 'through,' 'in,' 'over,' 'under,' etc.

And another thing!

Unpacking the shopping, finding a matching can, discussing what's in each packet or can, and where the items go, is a 'rich' experience.

First storybooks

What to do

Children will get maximum pleasure out of books if you add some drama! *The Three Billy Goats Gruff* is an example of a traditional book. First look through the pictures commenting on what you see. Then go back and read the story. Use a different voice for each goat and stamp your feet as they cross the bridge.

Try to link what you read to real life—a visit to a farm to see real goats or making oatmeal (porridge) before reading Goldilocks.

How it helps your child to learn

Reading is the No.1 priority to build vocabulary.

Reading Hints

- Use lots of sound effects and let him make them, too.
- Pause now and then and ask "I wonder what happens next?" Pause again—then say what you think happened.
- Look at **all** kinds of print—magazines, labels, catalogs, signs.
- Be enthusiastic as you read.
- Read every single day and at bedtime.
- Nursery rhyme books are good starters. Try some with associated audio-music cassettes, or video tapes, like *Snow White.*
- Favorite early authors: Dick Bruna, Dr. Seuss, Stan and Jan Berenstain, Richard Scarry.

Speech, reading, music

Special tip

Encourage him to take the lead. Explain things he points to. Repeat stories frequently.

And another thing!

You encourage a love of language by making books **fun**—which means varying your voice tone frequently and acting out parts.

The four types of words

What to do

Make sure you use at least four different types of words when talking to your child. Nouns, such as 'cat' and 'dog,' say what she can see. Verbs such as 'jump' and 'hop,' say what she can do. Adjectives, such as young and pretty, say how things look. And words such as slowly and quickly quantify actions or feelings.

How it helps your child to learn

Most children learn to speak nouns first and then verbs but it greatly increases their vocabulary to hear adjectives and adverbs. In this way, descriptions and feelings become part of their early understanding.

Speech, reading

Special tip

Put adverbs with simple verbs by asking your child to roll over *slowly*, turn *quickly*, dance *gently*, wash *thoroughly*.

And another thing!

Ask regularly about feelings, "How do you feel about that: happy or sad?" "Why is the cat purring? He sounds happy?"

Starting to make choices

What to do

During the early walking stage each child learns to make choices. And it's a good time for you to guide choices that are sensible. Whether a child eats an orange or an apple is a reasonable choice. If she's tired, it's not sensible to ask her whether she wants to go to bed or stay up. But a sensible choice would be to ask her which book she would like to read before she sleeps.

How it helps your child to learn

Making choices helps develop confidence, common sense and logic.

Thinking, confidence

Special tip

Offer your child the choice of which clothes to wear or which color ribbons to wear in her hair.

And another thing!

Where choices involve money, give plenty of time. "Which ice cream would you like? But choose carefully as we can't send it back."

The all-purpose plastic pail

What to do

Inexpensive plastic pails are favorites at any young age. Children can take them everywhere: to the beach for making sand castles; to the park for general play; outside to pick up leaves, sticks and twigs; in a home sandpit; and anywhere for treasure hunts. Keep other plastic items handy which can be used at the same time: small plastic spades, building blocks, spoons and empty plastic yogurt cups for stacking.

How it helps your child to learn

Something as simple as a plastic bucket will provide hours of creative fun and hand eye coordination for throwing.

Creativity

Special tip

Water play is particularly creative — transferring water by pail from one tub to another, or mixing it with sand, for instance.

And another thing!

Buckets are good for tossing games: throw acorns, walnuts and pine cones and count how many land in the pail and how many miss.

The curiosity walk

What to do

Regularly take your child out into your garden, into city parks or squares, nearby park or 'nature walk'. But don't hurry. Encourage him to look at everything, to listen to all the sounds, to touch different textures of stones, flowers and leaves, and to smell. Let him feel rain on his face, wind in his hair and comment on how it feels. Look at what fascinates him and build on those interests.

How it helps your child to learn

The more your child explores with all his senses, the more he learns. And the more you build on his interests, the better his knowledge base.

All senses & curiosity

Special tip

Volunteer information on the features that interest him. "That's a fern. A tiny green fern. That's a beautiful red rose. Smell it."

And another thing!

So long as it's safe and appropriate, encourage him to touch, taste and smell all the things that fascinate him.

Rhyme and rhythm

What to do

By the time your child is one, or earlier if you feel comfortable, introduce him to rhyming stories or cassettes: *Three Blind Mice, Jack and Jill, Humpty Dumpty* and *The Three Little Pigs*. Dr. Seuss rhyming beginner books are great. If you can play the piano, introduce him to *Twinkle, Twinkle, Little Star*.

How it helps your child to learn

Much language is imbedded in rhyme and rhythm. An early grounding provides the basis for poetry, music and also for enjoying the cadence and rhythm of verse. It's a great memory aid, too.

Speech, music, reading

Special tip

Seuss books such as *The Cat in The Hat* encourage reading as they repeat a limited vocabulary so it can be easily remembered.

And another thing!

You don't always need a book for nursery rhymes. Reciting one without a book helps a child develop his imagination.

Playing the name game

What to do

Your child will soon learn to recognize the sound of familiar names: Mommy, Daddy, Teddy, bottle and the parts of his body. We've included some nouns with this program. So as soon as you feel he knows the sounds of the early nouns, show him the written words too. Tell him distinctly what each one means, pointing to the object.

How it helps your child to learn

It's as easy for a child to learn to read a word as it is for him to speak it, so long as it is big enough for his young 'visual pathways' to take in.

nose

ball

The nouns included with *First FUNdamentals*, are enough for your child to begin to understand the basic idea of what reading means.

The *FUNdamentals* program for older infants includes a complete set of the 450 most used words and dozens of games that will enable your child to read competently before school.

Reading

Special tip

Ensure that the written noun is always directly related to the physical object, eg: "Here's Daddy's nose—and this is your ball."

And another thing!

Nouns are generally the best words to start with, particularly the names of parts of the child's own body which are very easy to identify.

Wallpaper 'Artwork'

What to do

Spread a large offcut of wallpaper out on the floor. Then give your child a chubby crayon and let her scribble on it. The sheer size invites what are actually pre-writing exercises.

How it helps your child to learn

It encourages early fine motor control and a recognition of cause (the scribble) and effect (the colors on the paper).

Pre-writing skills, creativity

Special tip

If she will stay still, you can trace her outline on the paper and show her her picture—filling in the details of her face, fingers, etc.

And another thing!

She can also 'paint' with pure water on a path on a hot day, and then watch the painting disappear!

An action song a day

What to do

Use any of the popular action songs —there are many on audio tapes, eg *Round and Round the Garden.* Say the rhyme with the actions a few times and pause just before the exciting finish and exaggerate your own actions.

How it helps your child to learn

Action songs stimulate a baby's:

- Sense of rhythm
- Ability to listen carefully
- Ability to predict
- Vocabulary

And learning in an affectionate and happy atmosphere builds trust.

An example of a good typical action song is:

This is the way the ladies ride Trip trop, trip trop, trip trop	Bounce quickly up and down on your knee.
This is the way the gentlemen ride Gall-op, gall-op, gall-op	Bounce slower but more vigorously
This is the way the farmer rides Hobble-dee, hobble-dee	Bounce from side to side.
Down into a ditch	Open your legs and let baby slide down.

Other good action songs are:

- Row Row Row the boat
- To market to market
- Ride a cock horse
- Rub-a-dub-dub
- Humpty Dumpty
- Pat-a-cake

Physical skills, language

Special tip

Let baby face you so she can see your expressions as well as the actions. Later face a mirror so she can see both of you.

And another thing!

You can later act out the rhymes with soft toys or finger puppets. Include songs like *Pat-a-cake,* so he joins in, too. Then he feels competent.

Finding things

What to do

Ask your baby to bring you an object she knows the name of, but which is out of sight, eg: a mug from a cupboard, or an object from a container.

Extend the game by putting different fruits on the table and pick one out saying "This is an orange. Can you find me an orange like this?" You can also use different types of toy farm animals, silverware, vegetables, toys.

THIS IS AN ORANGE, CAN YOU FIND ME AN ORANGE LIKE THIS?

How it helps your child to learn

It extends vocabulary, builds comprehension and starts one of the basic skills of mathematics, which is matching and sorting.

Vocabulary, classifying

Special tip

Be really clear—touch the object, and if necessary guide your baby's hand to the matching object.

And another thing!

Once your child can **match** (which is this game), you can get him to **sort** "put all the apples together" or sort leaves and pebbles in the garden.

Wiggly walk

What to do

Make out an interesting curved pathway on the floor for your child to walk along, eg: stepping stones made from old (non shiny) magazine pages. Explain that this is a path and go over it a few times together. Make a big fuss when she does it alone.

How it helps your child to learn

Develops the understanding that concentration and careful effort are needed to succeed. Later let her plan the route of the walk. Show her paths when you are out, and discuss what they are for and where they go.

Concentration, physical coordination

Special tip

You can hold her hand to start with. Later the walk can lead round the corner to where a favorite toy is hiding.

And another thing!

The wiggly walk can develop into an obstacle course, with cushions to navigate and chairs and tables to walk under.

Bathtime fun

Bathtime is **full** of rich possibilities. Let her:

1 Catch floating toys in a soup ladle.

2 Bath and shampoo a doll, talking about the parts of its body, wrapping it in a flannel, then drying it, and putting it to bed.)

3 Pour water from one container to another. Use yogurt pots, plastic bottles, jugs and pans. Talk about 'pour,' 'float,' 'full,' 'empty,' 'half full,' 'spill,' etc.

4 Point out the different sounds, dripping, running, splashing, bubbling, etc. Use a straw to blow air into water in a container. Compare a dry and wet sponge.

5 Let her experience different sensations of cold, hot, warmer.

Curiosity, respect for others

Special tip

Allow her to fill and empty the bath—supervising the hot water tap, of course. Find out which things float or sink.

And another thing!

Caring for a doll or toy is an essential way to develop sympathy and emotions.

Feelings plates

What to do

You'll need 6-8 large white paper plates. Use a marker pen to draw a separate face on each plate—smiling, sleeping, surprised, crying, laughing, sad, angry, yawning. Take each plate separately and mimic the expression on the face. Do it with exaggerated sounds, words and facial expressions. Tell him what you are doing. "I'm sad." "I'm happy."

How it helps your child to learn

The more he can appreciate other people's feelings, the better he will understand his own.

Self-esteem, emotions

Special tip

It's important to acknowledge feelings openly—even if they are not desirable as later behavior!

And another thing!

Help her express and then direct her emotions positively. "Cathy is angry because Alexander took her toy. Let's ask for it back."

Four important tips for play

1. Always think carefully about the amount of help you give your child. It should be enough to help him succeed **and no more**. The more he succeeds at even the simplest game on his own, the more he will build his self confidence.

   By the same token, consider how to make a game easier if he can't yet succeed at it. Building the feeling that if he tries he can succeed, is your number one priority.

2. Always comment on what you are doing. Use simple language to describe what she is seeing, as she is seeing it. That way she builds language and understands better what to do.

3. When he has mastered a game, think how you can make it more challenging.

   If he is comfortable with push-along toys with wheels, let him try pushing toys without wheels, such as building blocks and pans. When he can push these along, let him try what happens when he pushes them up and down a ramp. A 'rich' environment is one that includes fun challenges.

   If he is learning to throw, you might stand behind him and take his arm through the throwing motion saying "Throw" as he should let go of the ball. Then you would throw a soft foam ball or bean bag to him and ask him to throw it back.

   Then you would suggest he aims at something — say an open door or onto a large cushion — or even to knock a toy over.

   Finally, when he succeeds at throwing through a door, make the targets smaller—using a washing basket or bucket. Or use several balls and count how many he can get in.

   A progressively more challenging environment, which also produces success, builds a feeling of competence.

4. Encourage him with words that let him know **how** he is doing—not just simple praise or criticism.

   So "Well done, you looked carefully as you threw it." provides guidance on how to succeed. "Good boy" is not only unspecific praise, it can encourage him to do things to please you, not to please himself. The difference is subtle but important.

FIRST FUNDAMENTALS™

accelerated learning

Your *Big Noun* set

Your infant can learn written words at the same time as he learns spoken words. Even if he is too young to speak, he can take information in through his eyes and ears at the same time. So when he hears the word "ball" and sees the word "ball" at the same time he is learning to both speak and read. So start by labeling things that your child can see around the house: a bath, bed, cup.

Then show him the words for the parts of his body, saying, as you touch his nose, "This is your nose," and–pointing to the word nose, "Nose." Here are some examples to get you started. You can make other cards yourself with the names of pets or friends. But keep the letters as big as these samples.

ball

bed

book

cat

cup

eyes

foot

hand

hat

milk

nose